An Examination Of A
Disquieting, Disturbing,
Even Shocking,
Social, Business, Political, & Legal
Point-Based Rating System
For Determining Good & Bad Businesses & Citizens

The Chinese Social-Credit System Experience

A National Reputation System In The Making!

And What Can Result From These Ratings!

By Robert Netkin

Mountain View, California
July 2018

Robert Netkin
1375 Montecito Avenue #32
Mountain View, Ca. 94043
Phone: 650-962-0720

e-mail: rnetkin@pacbell.net
LinkedIn
twitter: Robert Netkin@rncreativewritr

Copyright Protected July 2018. Robert Netkin

All rights reserved. No part of this book may be reproduced or utilized in any form, or by any means; electronic, mechanical or otherwise; without expressed written permission.

Note:
There were no blocking firewalls or paid subscriptions required to access any of the cited source material.

Table Of Contents

Part One: Initial Exposure To The Chinese Social-Credit System   Pages 5-8

Rodion Ebbighausen
"China Experiments With Sweeping Social Credit System"
Pages 6-7

Part Two: How The Chinese Social-Credit System
Is Envisioned To Function – How It Is Indeed Functioning   Pages 9-15

Severine Arsene
"Trust In Ratings – China's Social Credit System"
Pages 9-12
Meg Jing Zeng
"China's Social Credit System Puts Its People Under Pressure
        To Be Model Citizens"
Pages 12-15

Part Three: The System In More Detail:
        The Long History Behind Its Implementation   Pages 16-69

Simina Mistreanu
"Life Inside China's Social Credit Laboratory"
Pages 16-21
Rogier Creemers
"China's Social Credit System: An Evolving Practice Of Control"
Pages 21-45
Martin Li
"A Pioneer Of China's Credit System"
(The Story of Huang Wenyun)
Pages 45-48
Lin Junyue
"Retrospect: 1999-2009 Achievements In Social Credit System
        Construction Of China"
Pages 49-67
Sara Hsu
"China's New Social Credit System"
Pages 67-69

Part Four: The Chinese Social Credit System At Work   Pages 70-140

Wikipedia
"Social Credit System"
Pages 70-75
Rogier Creemers' Editing & Translation of the State Council document:
"Planning Outline For The Construction
    Of A Social Credit System (2014-2020)"
Pages 76-107
Mirjam Meissner
"China's Social Credit System"
Pages 108-122
Mareike Ohlberg, Shazeda Ahmed, Bertram Lang
"Central Planning, Local Experiments"
Pages 123-140

Part Five: A Closer Examination Of Potential Implications   Pages 141-152

Dom Galeon, Brad Bergan
"China's 'Social Credit System' Will Rate
    How Valuable You Are As A Human"
Pages 141-144
Stefan Brehm, Nicholas Loubere
"China's Dystopian Social Credit System
    Is A Harbinger Of The Global Age Of The Algorithm"
Pages 145-147
Amulya Shankar
"What's Your Citizen 'Trust Score'?
China Moves To Rate Its 1.3 Billion Citizens"
(Featuring an interview with author Rachel Botsman)
Pages 148-150
John Harris
"The Tyranny Of Algorithms Is Part Of Our Lives:
    Soon They Could Rate Everything We Do"
Pages 150-152

This Examination Of China's Social Credit System Brought To A Close
Pages 153-154

Part One:
Initial Exposure To The Chinese Social-Credit System

It's late June 2018 and I'm flipping through channels on my TV, and I come across DW (Deutsche Welle) TV's presentation of a regularly scheduled Global 3000 episode, on one of the local Northern California public TV stations. The show happens to be featuring a relatively in-depth segment about something referred to as China's developing social point/credit system.

To say the least, the segment certainly has a strong and highly memorable impact – in a disquieting, disturbing, even shocking way, as the implications for personal privacy, individual choice, and perhaps even critical, independent thinking, not-so-slowly sinks in!

Thinking way back, to a much earlier time in life, such a point system seems okay – in a lower-level school setting, with credits and points (or stars) given for things like good test performance and especially good behavior; and demerits or deductions in points for bad behavior, or more lame explanations for absences. But on a society-wide basis – with somewhere around 1.4 billion Chinese people potentially involved; well, I was quick to see that the implementation of such a social-credit system warranted considerably more investigation, and quickly, at that!

Yes; that such a social-credit system, as it is known, could be well along in development, was just too stunning, even shocking, with so many potential implications, to be simply shrugged off, and allowed to go by with hardly a serious notice, without a lot closer examination!

And so this project: "The Chinese Social-Credit Experience: A National Reputation System In The Making", was quickly begun. And in relatively short order – this is the result.

Most of the source material is of highly recent derivation: mid-2017 to mid-2018, with the exception of most of the background material which set the stage for these latest developments, which range in origin from the mid-1990s to 2015 or so.

Historically of course, all that is to be considered very recent, and indicative of the fact that such developments are only in their earliest stages, fundamentally because such a more widespread "reputation" system could only be initiated with the availability of widespread computer interconnectivity, massive data storage availability, and immense calculating capability and capacity.

Because I doubt there is anything like "widespread" and in-depth knowledge about the Chinese system, and the tremendous implications of the development and existence of such a system; and the on-going steady roll-out and implementation of such a socially all-inclusive and wide-ranging system even now requiring the participation of so many millions – even billions of people; getting involved in this project, in order to bring more of the details of the development of China's social-credit system to many more people seemed – now seems, even more imperative!

A good beginning point for telling this story is the article titled "China Experiments With Sweeping Social Credit System – China Wants To Introduce A Social Credit System To Rate Its Citizens Trustworthiness. Unconcerned About Privacy Protection, The Government Is Billing The Project As A Cure For All Manner Of Economic And Social Ills." The author is Rodion Ebbighausen; and it is article a-42030727 on www.dw.com/en, and is dated April 1, 2018.

The article begins:

"Are you a good person? In the event that you're not quite sure, help will soon be at hand in China. The government there is planning to introduce a comprehensive rating system for its citizens, known as the Social Credit System. In addition to scoring a person's credit worthiness, it will also gather and evaluate information on social behavior.

People who don't visit their aging parents regularly, for example, will get minus points. The same goes for people who cross the street on a red light or illegally dump their garbage. And in the city of Zhengzhou, people who don't respond to a court order will be reminded of that fact every time they answer their phone.

Those are just three examples of around 40 different experiments the Chinese government is trying out at the municipal level to find out how best to implement the planned Social Credit System.

Wide-reaching Data Machine

The state Social Credit System will link existing data from registry offices or school officials, in addition to customer ratings from apps and people's online activity. It will also incorporate automatically generated data, for example from video surveillance systems with help from facial recognition."

It's a social-credit system – and experiment, that the government in Beijing made the decision to introduce in 2014.

Naming And Shaming

At the system's core is the punishment of wrongdoers and the rewarding of model citizens. Under the parts of the system already in place today, people deemed to be 'untrustworthy' are not allowed to buy tickets for flights or high-speed trains or send their children to private schools, for example. The private pay system Sesame Credit has been giving the Chinese a taste of what's to come. In 2016, it registered 7.3 million cases of instances where it had blocked flight bookings for people with poor ratings. There are also experiments that give tax breaks to model citizens or easier customs processes to trustworthy companies." And "The experiments with the Social Credit System are set to continue until 2020, when the system will be implemented nationwide. New experiments will also be added, and evaluated."

The article continues by noting that Bjorn Alpermann, an expert on China at the University of Wurzburg, "thinks that full-scale implementation will take a few years, especially given the fact that such a system requires enormous investment. But once implementation is complete, will China begin to export its comprehensive citizen surveillance system? 'I can imagine that the Chinese government would someday sell the technology behind this project to another authoritarian regime,' said Alpermann – an impression bolstered by Chinese President Xi Jinping's recent tendency to promote the project internationally as a forward-looking alternative."

A Little Historical Perspective

An experiment, a massive effort, like creating a social-credit system – the need for the Chinese (leadership & people) to want to, to feel it necessary and desirable, to establish something like a national reputation system, comes with long and strong philosophical, legal, social, cultural and political ideologies and perspectives, leading up to it – of that there can be no doubt!

The reality is that something like the establishment of a modern-day social-credit system doesn't just pop out of people's minds from nowhere – there has to be a long story behind it; and there has to be very much modern-day resources to support, to provide the backbone, the infrastructure, for its implementation!

How such a social-credit credit system is envisioned; how it actually functions; the long history and modern-day people behind its implementation; the plan itself and its rollout towards 2020; the implications of such a system; the technology behind it; advocators claimed/perceived strengths and critics/opponents claimed/perceived flaws, weaknesses, and dangers of such a system; its global fit and potential – these are all parts of the important story that needs telling – NOW!

Part Two:
How The Chinese Social-Credit System Is Envisioned To Function – How It is Indeed Functioning

An Overview

"Trust In Ratings: China's Social Credit System" – is an article posted by AsiaGlobal Online on May 17, 2018, and was written by Severine Arsene, holder of PhD in Political Science – Sciences Po Paris and Managing Director AsiaGlobal Online, at the Asia Global Institute, The University of Hong Kong.

The article begins:
"China is looking to restore 'trust' and 'sincerity' in society by making a digital 'social credit system.' In this kaleidoscopic system of ratings and blacklists, good deeds are met with rewards, and bad deeds with punishments. China hopes this will cure many current ailments, including corruption in government procurement, a lack of food security, and unequal access to healthcare. But the rest of the world can also learn something from this project: namely, the dangers of governing by grading people.

When Communist-Style Social Control Meets Post-Modern Governance

The compilation of digital files on individuals may be seen as a revival of the principle of 'dang'an', a file containing one's school, work and political records. The dang'an has lost a lot of its impact on urban citizens' lives with the advent of the market economy. But with its aim of sharing data across administrative sectors, the social credit system may bring new life to the device.

The dang'an aside, a key idea behind the social credit system is that economic development is hampered by a lack of 'trust' within society. There is a real need in China for reliable financial credit data to make loans and transactions more secure. Thus the plan for the system puts great emphasis on economic misbehavior, such as failing to pay one's bills.

But from a citizen's perspective, the social credit system, the way it is envisioned to function and the way it's been functioning as it's been rolled out, takes the reality of this experiment to a whole new level of what could well be considered 'intrusiveness.' In this iteration, a person's 'social trustworthiness' depends on more than just interactions with public authorities or financial capabilities. Even their personal, intimate behavior is part of the criteria.

Good Social Credit Means Perks

What makes this system particularly effective is that it aligns credit ratings with everyday benefits for citizens. In pilot municipalities like Rongcheng in Shandong province, the social credit system is incorporated into a reorganization of public services. A good credit rating entitles one to discounts on utilities, favorable loan rates, and waivers on deposits for bike rentals. Indeed, residents have enjoyed more safety on the roads, as drivers and pedestrians adhere to rules for fear of losing credit points.

On the other side, people who lose credit face disproportionate punishments. For instance, the Supreme People's Court blacklists individuals for failing to repay their debts and prohibits them from traveling by plane or first-class trains. More importantly, these people's names and personal details are published for everyone to see on a web portal. This blacklist can be picked up by the credit rating services, creating ripples across different aspects of the subjects' lives, extending to their families and friends.

This is where the social credit system differs from the old, secret dang'an. One's social credit rating is meant to be open to the public. In principle," usage of companies rating services, such as Ant Financial's "Sesame Credit, is voluntary: customers need to opt in to get a rating. In exchange, it offers a wide range of benefits, such as fast-tracked visa applications and easier car rental. Just like how it is so hard to leave Facebook even after the Cambridge Analytica scandal, the advantages offered by these (rating) services make it very costly for users in China to opt out. The subtle yet coercive power of reputation in social networks thus spreads throughout people's daily lives.

The Pitfalls Of Governance By Ratings

According to the official planning outline, the social credit system is intended to 'stimulate the development of society and the progress of civilization.' But the criteria on which individuals are judged are largely determined by the localities, administrations and businesses that put pilot programs in place. This means that Chinese citizens are not held to uniform standards – it all depends on where they live and what platforms they use.

In effect, the criteria tend to bundle moral and political values together with laws and regulations. In Rongcheng, a citizen can be rewarded for being a good daughter-in-law or giving to charity. Sesame Credit is said to take into account consuming patterns such as purchasing diapers (a good thing), and entertainment habits such as playing online games (a bad thing). In most cases, credit systems reward very conservative values and conformist behavior. They also tend to discriminate against the poor, by rewarding consumption, and by putting particular emphasis on penalizing 'deadbeat borrowers' and those who cannot pay their utility bills on time.

Citizens have little say in the definition of criteria, despite the pervasive impact the social credit system has on their lives. In Suining county in Jiangsu province, an early pilot program assigned the population to four categories, A to D, according to obscure criteria. It triggered strong opposition from the population and had to be revamped. This case shows that technology doesn't guarantee fairness, nor can it preempt resistance.

Cybersecurity And Technical Issues

And then there are the risks brought about by the technologies themselves, vulnerability to hacking and database breakdown being the most obvious. In addition, making myriad databases interoperable is an enormous challenge. Even if that could be overcome, there's still the matter of data accuracy. The input and handling of data are prone to errors. If all social credit databases were linked, erroneous data in any one database would be replicated across different platforms.

The people in charge of these systems find themselves in an unusual position of power. Without strong checks in place, there will be new opportunities for political surveillance, industrial espionage, and even blackmail and bribery.

Governance By Algorithms Requires Democratic Oversight

The all-encompassing scope of the social credit system has incited an endless stream of dystopian commentaries." (Note: dystopian equates to anti-utopian, to something like a place, a community or society where people lead dehumanized, fearful lives, often in a totalitarian or post-apocalyptic world like Aldous Huxley's 1932 "Brave New World".) "Observers in other countries wonder to copy or fight it. Some worry about possible extraterritorial effects, as foreign entities active in China may be ranked too, and as private companies are increasingly using the same tools to regulate access to public spaces."

Conclusions reached are: "Challenges do remain. Implementing a countrywide social credit system that actually works will be an enormous technical and bureaucratic challenge. Moreover, pervasive surveillance may generate complications that could undermine social stability. What is sure is that experimentation of this type and scale is unprecedented.

The world can learn from China's social credit system what is at stake when governance is done through data collection and algorithmic ratings. We tend to underestimate how much of this is already going on around the world. For instance, U.S. agencies collect intrusive personal data to allocate and distribute welfare benefits, and they do so using biased algorithms that effectively increase inequalities.

The social credit system should thus be a wake-up call. The world should acknowledge that data-processing technologies are political devices. They must be considered, transparent, and have strong and effective checks and balances."

Another important article is "China's Social Credit System Puts Its People Under Pressure To Be Model Citizens". It was written by Meg Jing Zeng, PhD candidate, Queensland University Of Technology, Brisbane, Australia, and is dated January 23, 2018, and can be found posted online on The Conversation.com

The article begins:
"In less than a month, China's Lunar New Year will bring the country's annual epic travel rush – the largest human migration on earth. While many are planning trips to their home towns to attend family reunions, millions more Chinese citizens have been blacklisted by authorities, labeled as 'not qualified' to book flights or high-speed train tickets.

This citizen ranking and blacklisting mechanism is a pilot scheme of China's Social Credit System. With a mission to 'raise the awareness of integrity and the level of trustworthiness of Chinese society', the Chinese government is planning to launch the system nationwide by 2020 to rate the trustworthiness of its 1.4 billion citizens.

What 'Credit' Means In China

The word 'credit' in Chinese – xinyong – is a core tenet of traditional Confucian ethics, which can be traced back to the late 4th century B.C. In its original context, xinyong is a moral concept that indicates one's honesty and trustworthiness. In the past few decades, its meaning has been extended to include financial creditworthiness.

So what does 'credit' mean in the Social Credit System?

It is a question Chinese authorities have been exploring for more than 10 years. When the plan of constructing a Social Credit System was first proposed in 2007, the primary goal was to restore market order by leveraging the financial creditworthiness of businesses and individuals.

Gradually the scope of the project has infiltrated other aspects of daily life.

Actions that can now harm one's personal credit record include not showing up to a restaurant without having cancelled the reservation, cheating in online games, leaving false product reviews, and jaywalking.

Reaping Rewards For 'Good Deeds'

One shared focus of the country's existing pilot schemes is to generate a standardised reward and punishment system based on a citizen's credit score.

Most pilot cities have used a points system, whereby everyone starts off with a baseline of 100 points. Citizens can earn bonus points up to the value of 200 by performing 'good deeds', such as engaging in charity work or separating and recycling rubbish. In Suzhou city, for example, one can earn six points for donating blood.

Being a 'good citizen' is well rewarded. In some regions, citizens with high social credit scores can enjoy free gym facilities, cheaper public transport, and shorter wait times in hospitals. Those with low scores, on the other hand, may face restrictions to their travel and public service access.

At this stage, scores are connected to a citizen's identification card number. But the Chinese internet court has proposed an online identification system connected to social media accounts.

Naming And Shaming Of Blacklisted Citizens

Publishing the details of blacklisted citizens online is a common practice, but some cities choose to take public shaming to another level.

Several provinces have been using TV and LED screens in public spaces to expose people. In some regions authorities have remotely personalised the dial tones of blacklisted debtors so that callers will hear a message akin to: 'the person you are calling is a dishonest debtor.'

It is important for a country to be able to enforce court orders, but when the judicial and legislative systems sometimes malfunction, as they do in China, it raises questions about whether the ability to expose and punish without due process can lead to abuses of power.

Liu Hu, a vocal journalist who has criticised government officials on social media, was accused of 'spreading rumour and defamation'. While seeking legal redress in early 2017, he realised that he was blacklisted as 'untrustworthy' and prohibited from purchasing plane tickets.

Liu's story may be an isolated incident, but it demonstrates how the system could potentially be used to push the government's agenda and to crack down on dissent.

Harnessing The Power Of Big Data

The role of big data in the project has received broad media attention outside China due to concerns about how the Chinese government may use its power to further intensify surveillance.

For example, Chinese tech giants Alibaba and Tencent are testing user credit files based on behavioural data gathered through people's use of social media and e-commerce sites. To date, few operational details have been released about the country's plan to integrate user data from online platforms into a central system overseen by the government.

This will soon change. Since last December, the National Development and Reform Commission and Central Bank of China began to approve pilot plans to integrate big data with the Social Credit System. As one of China's first pilot provinces, Guizhou was selected to showcase a government-led experiment of a big data-empowered Social Credit System.

Guizhou is one of the poorest provinces in China, and is mostly known for being the home of Maotai – a high-quality liquor. This seemingly random choice of location is actually tactical. Unbeknown to most, since 2015 this rural backwater has been fast becoming the country's hub of big data.

In 2017, tech giants Google, Microsoft, Baidu, Huawei and Alibaba established research facilities and data centres in the region. In 2018, Apple is following suit and transferring its Chinese iCloud server to a local company.

Guizhou's position as the country's data centre makes it an ideal social laboratory for the local government's Social Credit System experiments.

Turning The System Back On The Government

While some might view China's Social Credit System as something out of dystopian fiction, if properly implemented the system can have positive impacts – especially when used to keep government officials and business owners accountable.

Most pilot schemes target companies as stringently as individuals. Firms with a history of environmental damage or product safety concerns are now regularly exposed on online blacklists.

Government officials can also be found on online blacklists. As of December 2017, more than 1,100 government officials had been blacklisted as untrustworthy. Such a move to expose corruption is arguably more beneficial to Chinese society than public shaming of jaywalkers.

As Professor Du Liqun of Peking University argues, in the Chinese context the construction of a Social Credit System should start with building a trustworthy government."

Note: I have to interject about the blacklisting of government officials: skeptically, and somewhat cynically speaking, the big problem with such blacklisting, is how to know if there isn't some highly political basis for such actions, such as the carefully-focused eliminating of a political opponent, rather than proven corruption? And the same can be said of businesses – how can it be known that a company hasn't been "framed", to increase its difficulty of engaging in fair competition? It's not hard to see how such a system could be "gamed" to benefit one politician or company over another! I'd imagine such considerations have already arisen, but I don't think I've seen much material to explain how such riggings of the system can be determined and handled judiciously and expeditiously – other than trusting the system, and the fair and expeditious handling of judicial appeals (which I've seen relatively little evidence to suggest that would frequently be the case!). But of course I could be wrong - and offer sincere apologies, if such is, in fact, the case!

Part Three:
The System In More Detail:
The Long History Behind Its Implementation

This part of the story is about the modern-day people - the architects, the designers, behind the system; those who were influential in creating its architecture – how it is designed, and what it is intended to do; and who also are significantly involved in overseeing the system's implementation.

And it begins with a Foreign Policy.com "Dispatch", written by Simina Mistreanu – a Beijing-based journalist, who got her Master's degree in Journalism from the University Of Missouri, after growing up in Romania and doing her early work as a journalist there, before coming to the U.S. in 2011. This article is dated April 3, 2018, and titled, "Life Inside China's Social Credit Laboratory", and subtitled, "The Party's Massive Experiment In Ranking And Monitoring Chinese Citizens Has Already Started"; and Cai Yinan and Wu Xiaoxi are credited with contributing reporting.

Ms. Mistreanu begins her story in what is now the familiar location of Rongcheng, China. And after a short peek into Rongcheng and the local functioning of China's Social Credit System, Ms. Mistreanu begins offering more of an overview, with, "By 2020, the government has promised to roll out a national social credit system. According to the system's founding document, released by the State Council in 2014, the scheme should 'allow the trustworthy to roam everywhere under heaven while making it hard for the discredited to take a single step.' But at a when the Chinese Communist Party is aggressively advancing its presence across town hall offices and company boardrooms, this move has sparked fears that it is another step in the tightening of China's already scant freedoms."

Note: of course that is a highly subjective viewing of the situation in China concerning "freedom" – not necessarily, from an outsider's point of view, a wrong "conclusion"; but, I'm guessing, one not-so-likely to be shared by as many Chinese citizens as would be expected!

Ms. Mistreanu continues, "But it has been hard to distinguish future promises – or threats – from the realities of how social credit is being implemented. Rongcheng is one place where that future is visible. Three dozen pilot systems have been rolled out in cities across the country, and Rongcheng is one of them."

And the system includes not only citizens. Ms. Mistreanu writes, "Companies are also included in the gauntlet of social credit. They can remain in good standing if they pay taxes on time and avoid fines for things such as substandard or unsanitary products – a

16

sore point for Chinese people, who tend to mistrust firms and service providers due to frequent scams and food safety scandals. High-scoring businesses pass through fewer hoops in public tenders and get better loan conditions."

Ms. Mistreanu continues her overview, "Rongcheng is a microcosm of what is to come. The national credit system planned for 2020 will be an 'ecosystem' made up of schemes of various sizes and reaches, run by cities, government ministries, online payment providers, down to neighborhoods, libraries, and businesses, say Chinese researchers who are designing the national scheme. It will all be interconnected by an invisible web of information.

But contrary to some western press accounts, which often confuse existing private credit systems with the future schemes, it will not be a unified platform where one can type in his or her ID and get a single three-digit score that will decide their lives. This caricature of a system that doles out unique scores to 1.4 billion people could not work technically nor politically, says Rogier Creemers, a scholar of Chinese law at the Leiden University Institute for Area Studies in the Netherlands."

Note: Rogier Creemers' name is a very important one, since it will come up many times in this examination of the Chinese Social Credit System. In fact his name is attached to the English translation of the founding documents of the Social Credit System, as well to a highly significant and in-depth examination of the system itself - with more about both still to come. Yes, a lot more about Rogier Creemers is still to come!

Returning to Ms. Mistreanu's narrative, "The system would instead expand and automatize existing forms of bureaucratic control, formalizing the existing controls and monitoring of Chinese citizens.

'The social credit system is just really adding technology and adding a formality to the way the party already operates,' says Samantha Hoffman, a consultant at the International Institute for Strategic Studies (IISS) who researches Chinese social management.

The Communist party has experimented with forms of social control ever since it came to power in 1949, though China's self-policing tradition stretches back to the Song dynasty. An 11th-century emperor instituted a grid system where groups of 5 to 25 households kept tabs on each other and were empowered to arrest delinquents.

But previous efforts largely focused on groups, not individuals. As early as the 1950s, during Mao Zedong's rule, rural Chinese were forced into communes that farmed collectively – to disastrous effect – and had their status measured as a group. Similarly 'danwei' were work units whose members were apportioned public goods and were ranked based on their 'good' or 'bad' political standing. Such groups were supposed to police their own members – efforts inevitably tied to the violent political struggles of the Maoist era.

Post 1980s, the state relied on hukou, or housing registration, to keep tabs on where people lived, worked, and sent their children to school. But the hukou system often broke down when confronted with China's mass urbanization in recent decades, which saw hundreds of millions of migrant workers move into metropolises despite poor access to housing and social services.

Along with society at large, the Communist Party has always monitored its own members for both ideological and personal loyalties. E-government projects that started in the 1990s, such as the Golden Shield, which connected public security bureaus across the country through an online network, have been aimed at both efficiency and control.

Former President Jiang Zemin in 1995 called for 'the informatization, automation, and intelligentization of economic and social management.' In the early 2000s, his successor, Hu Jintao, attempted to automate social surveillance through modern grid policing projects in cities such as Shanghai. Hu, with his minister of public security, Zhou Yongkang, dreamed up a monitoring system capable of functioning automatically, with the end goal being to keep the Communist Party in power.

The result of decades of control, however, is that Chinese society suffers from a lack of trust, says veteran sociologist Zhang Lifan. People often expect to be cheated or to get in trouble without having done anything. This anxiety, Zhang says, stems from the Cultural Revolution (1966-1976), when friends and family members were pitted against one another and millions of Chinese were killed in political struggles.

'It's a problem the ruling party itself has created,' Zhang says, 'and now it wants to solve it.'

And Ms. Mistreanu continues, "In Beijing, Zhang Lili is one of the researchers designing the national social credit system. She works at Peking University's China Credit Research Center, which was established more than 15 years ago for this purpose.

Zhang ... talks about how the idea for the system originated in China's rapid economic expansion. It's a narrative commonly put forward in China: because the Chinese market economy didn't take centuries to expand like in the West, people need the government to keep companies and businesspeople in check, as well as to ensure a smooth urbanization.

The Peking University credit center started in the early 2000s with social credit projects for tourism agencies, the Ministry of Commerce, and academic researchers. The rankings were based on criteria such as permits and professional qualifications.

'But now with the inclusion of personal information, because there's more debate about it, (the government) is more cautious,' Zhang says.

The experience of an early citywide experiment might explain why. In 2010, authorities in Suining, a county in Jiangsu province near Shanghai, launched a pilot project that included criteria such as residents' education level, online behavior, and compliance with traffic laws. Locals would earn points for looking after elderly family members or helping the poor and lose them for minor traffic offenses or if they illegally petitioned higher authorities for help. High scorers were fast-tracked for job promotions and gained access to top schools, while those at the bottom were restricted from some permits and social services.

The scheme was a disaster. Both residents and state media blasted it for its seemingly unfair and arbitrary criteria, with one state-run newspaper comparing the system to the 'good citizen' certificates issued by Japan during its wartime occupation of China. The Suining pilot was cancelled but not before teaching the government some lessons about what is palatable to the public." Researcher Zhang's conclusion: "China needs a 'very delicate' type of administration."

Ms. Mistreanu writes, "As (the experience in) Rongcheng shows, enforcing the law is a priority of the social credit system. Chinese courts struggle to enforce their judgments, especially civil ones. They're hampered by their relatively low status in the political system, the country's sheer size and scale, and the varied and often contentious levels of law enforcement.

On the one hand, the scheme wants to address real problems that Chinese society is confronting, such as financial scams, counterfeit products, and unsanitary restaurants, which amount to a 'lack of trust in the market,' says Creemers of the Leiden Institute.

'Yes, the social credit system is connected with maintaining the integrity and stability of the political regime,' he says. 'It is also the case that it tries to do so by addressing legitimate concerns. And that complicates the criticism.'

Perhaps the most controversial initiative so far is a supreme court blacklist of 170,000 defaulters who are barred from buying high-speed train or airplane tickets or staying at luxury hotels as a means to pressure them to repay their debt.

The public blacklist has been incorporated by another incarnation of the social credit system – Zhima Credit, a service of the mobile payment provider Alipay. China has a huge mobile payment market, with transactions totaling $5.5 trillion in 2016, compared with $112 billion in the United States. Alipay, owned by Ant Financial, and WeChat Pay dominate the still-growing Chinese market.

Zhima Credit is an optional service embedded in Alipay that calculates users' personal credit based on data such as spending history, friends on Alipay's social network, and other types of consumer behavior. Zhima Credit's technology director told the Chinese magazine Caixin in 2015 that buying diapers, for example, would be considered 'responsible' behavior, while playing video games could be counted against you.

Hu Tao, Zhima Credit's general manager, paints a different picture now. She says the app doesn't monitor social media posts 'nor does it attempt to measure qualitative characteristics like character, honesty, or moral value.' Zhima Credit is not a pilot for the social credit system and doesn't share data with the government without users' consent, she says." But Ms. Mistreanu adds, "However, the company is blending into the invisible web of China's upcoming social credit system."

And Ms. Mistreanu writes, "There's no single institution in command of the social credit system. Instead, the web made of various schemes, stretches and blends; inching from the more popular restrictions for breaking laws to new, grayer areas. The National Development and Reform Commission, a powerful central body, said in March that it would extend train and flight travel restrictions for actions such as spreading false information about terrorism and using expired tickets.

The government will in the end have inordinate amounts of data at its disposal to control and intervene in society, politics, and the economy. This strategy is deliberate and well thought out, argues Sebastian Heilmann of the Mercator Institute for China Studies in Berlin. (Note: additional very significant work coming from other Mercator Institute contributors will be reviewed later!) 'With the help of Big Data, China's leadership strives to eliminate the flaws of Communist systems,' he (Mr. Heilmann) wrote in a Financial Times op-ed." And Ms. Mistreanu adds, "China's troves of data will help the government allocate resources, solve problems, and squelch dissent – or so, at least, the government hopes."

Ms. Mistreanu continues, "The unified social credit system will rally all sectors of society against those deemed untrustworthy, says author Murong Xuecun, who has had run-ins with the Chinese government because of his writings. Murong believes dissidents will experience a 'multifaceted punishment,' and more and more people will become cautious about their remarks.

'The Chinese government is increasingly inclined to use high tech to monitor ordinary people, turning China into a police state, a big prison,' says Zhang Lifan, the sociologist.

Zhang and Murong's voices, however, are so far exceptions. If people have doubts, they're not voicing them."

Ms. Mistreanu concludes with, "In the larger picture, the Communist Party is trying to stay in power 'by making China a pleasant and acceptable place for people to live in order to not get angry,' Creemers says. 'It doesn't mean it's benevolent. Keeping people happy is a much more effective means than employing force.'

The party is using both coercion and cooperation to integrate the scheme into people's lives and have it bring benefits to them. 'To me, that's what makes it Orwellian,' says Hoffman of IISS. The social credit system provides incentives for people to not want to be on a blacklist. 'It's a preemptive way of shaping the way people think and shaping the way people act,' she (Ms. Hoffman) says. And to the extent that people believe they can benefit socially and economically from the Communist Party staying in power, the system is working."

Moving on, the following comprehensive article, titled "China's Social Credit System: An Evolving Practice Of Control" is an essential source of information about this effort. The article is written by the previously introduced Rogier Creemers, of the University of Leiden – Van Vollenhoven Institute, is dated May 9, 2018; and has been uploaded from https:// SSRNsolutions.com – "an early stage research platform for connecting researchers, evolving ideas, and sharing research".

The highly detailed article begins with the following Abstract:

"The Social Credit System (SCS) is perhaps the most prominent manifestation of the Chinese government's intention to reinforce legal, regulatory and policy processes through the application of information technology. Yet its organizational specifics have not yet received academic scrutiny. This paper will identify the objectives, perspectives and mechanisms through which the Chinese government has sought to realize its vision of 'social credit'.

Reviewing the system's historical evolution, institutional structure, central and local implementation, and relationship with private sector, this paper concludes that it is perhaps more accurate to conceive of the SCS as an ecosystem of initiatives broadly sharing a similar underlying logic, than a fully unified and integrated machine for social control.

It also finds that, intentions with regards to big data and artificial intelligence notwithstanding, the SCS remains a relatively crude tool. This may change in the future and this paper suggests the dimensions to be studied in order to assess this evolution."

And Mr. Creemers goes into the widely foot-noted (which goes beyond the scope of this book, and so will not be offered in this study of the extensive) details of his paper:

"A major problem in China's legal reform efforts has been ensuring effective legal and regulatory implementation, enforcement and compliance. In areas ranging from the enforcement of civil judgments and intellectual property, to environmental protections and food safety, the phenomenon that 'enforcement is difficult' (zhixing nan) remains prominent.

The Chinese leadership has recognized this, identifying the improvement of implementation and compliance mechanisms as a key component of the legal reform agenda outlined at the 4th Plenum (special group meeting) of 2014. Partly, subsequent reform measures have focused on the incremental improvement of existing judicial and administrative mechanisms. A revision of the Administrative Litigation Law, combined with directives to the courts to accept more administrative cases, led to a considerable increase in the number of administrative cases accepted. The institution of circuit appeals courts reduced the dependence of the judiciary on local governments, while changes to the case filing system reduced the discretion courts had to accept and reject cases – a process often infused with issues of politics and corruption.

At the same time, the leadership has also explored the development of novel, technology-driven tools for social control, to supplement traditional means of governing state and society. The high priority of forestalling threats to the integrity of China's political system has fuelled an increasingly powerful security state. Surveillance and monitoring have become pervasive across China, particularly in politically sensitive areas such as Tibet and Xinjiang. Technology is increasingly introduced into the judicial system, to enhance the effectiveness of trial processes, and increase the transparency of judicial information. In urban areas, 'grid management' techniques integrate information and communication technologies with street-level policing, social services and both coercive and cooperative forms of management.

The objective is responding to social unrest, and preventing the materialization of potentially destabilizing risks. Here too, the use of technology has been central, encompassing the installation of increasingly sophisticated CCTV cameras, surveillance through mobile devices number plate recognition and facial recognition tools. Ambitious development plans also indicate the leadership's intention to further harness big data and artificial intelligence for the purpose of social management.

One social management programme that has gained particular prominence is the Social Credit System (shehui xinyong tixi – SCS)"; with the footnoted emphasis that "one linguistic note must be made: the Mandarin term 'credit' (xinyong) carries a wider meaning than its English language counterpart. It not only includes notions of financial ability to service debt, but is cognate with terms for sincerity, honesty and integrity."

And Mr. Creemers continues, "According to the planning document that outlines its most recent iteration (note: Planning Outline for The Construction of a Social Credit System (2014-2020) of June 14, 2014, which will be examined in much greater detail in this book) 'its inherent requirements are establishing the idea of a sincerity culture, and promoting honesty and traditional virtues, it uses encouragement for trustworthiness and constraints against untrustworthiness as incentive mechanisms, and its objective is raising the sincerity consciousness and credit levels of the entire society.'

In other words, the SCS is framed as a set of mechanisms providing rewards or punishments as feedback to actors, based not just on the lawfulness, but also the morality of their actions, covering economic, social and political conduct.

This maximalist objective, combined with China's rapidly increasing technological prowess, the absence of strong constitutional protections for individual citizens, and the turn towards stricter Party control under the Xi Jinping administration, have led numerous observers to portray the SCS as an Orwellian nightmare, where Big Brother and big data conspire to finally realize the totalitarian impulses of China's autocratic leaders.

In this vision, often compared with an episode of the dystopian television series 'Black Mirror' in which people continuously rate their interactions with one another, China will have established a comprehensive system by 2020. This will not only track the movements and actions of individual citizens, but also process them to result in a quantified score. This score would be based on data points including online purchases, posted content on social media, and the sort of friends one has. In turn, the score would have a wide-ranging impact on people's lives, influencing their ability to get jobs, loans and mortgages , their relationships with friends and family, and even their ability to travel.

The image such portrayals conjure up is one of an omnipotent behemoth relentlessly carrying out a long-prepared scheme for complete control. The question, however, is whether that assessment is justified, and if not, how the SCS does impact the direction of China's legal and governance reform. Exactly how does the SCS complement, reinforce or undermine the functioning of existing judicial and administrative law enforcement processes, which role does it play itself in the shaping of social rules and norms? More broadly…what sort of social control tool is the SCS meant to be, and how does the SCS designate different classes in Chinese society, and justify differentiated treatment?

The answer to these questions requires, first and foremost, a thorough study of the thinking and design processes behind the SCS, and providing this is the objective of this Article. It combines the extensive use of Chinese language source material, hitherto unutilized in English-language scholarly work, with observations from field visits to China in the period 2014-2017.

During this period, SCS-related initiatives are deployed simultaneously by multiple stakeholders, at various levels of government, in the public and private sectors, continuously learning off and influenced by each other. The idea originated first in the context of China's market economic reforms, where it was seen as a potential solution to the perceived lack of trustworthy and moral conduct resulting in abuses ranging from intellectual property infringement to the sale of adulterated foodstuffs.

Over time, its scope of application expanded as the leadership found the idea attractive in other areas of governance as well. There is a central core: the fundamental objective of the SCS is instituting cybernetic mechanisms of behavioral control, where individuals and organizations are monitored in order to automatically confront them with the consequences of their actions."

And Mr. Creemers continues, "While it builds on intellectual, ideological and structural antecedents already present in China's governance architecture, the SCS has undergone, and continues to undergo, a process of development which builds on, and feeds into, shifting governance priorities, new possibilities enabled by technological development, and the iterative learning process so typical of Chinese policymaking.

This paper consists of four sections. A first section will review the historical antecedents for the SCS. More specifically, it will discuss how the SCS is building on, and tactically borrowing from, a storehouse of ideas, concepts, approaches and techniques that has profoundly shaped Chinese political and legal practice in the past, sometimes dating back to imperial days.

The second section will trace the emergence and expansion of social credit-related notions at the central and local levels of the Party-State, as well as preliminary institutional steps taken to start constructing the system.

The third section will survey the 2014 Plan for the Construction of the Social Credit System, which remains the most comprehensive planning document in this field, as well as subsequent implementation measures and local trials. It will pay particular attention to the Joint Punishment System (lianhe chengzhi tixi), the first major element of the SCS to enter into nationwide service.

The fourth section shifts the attention from the state to the private sector: spurred on by policies to develop tools to measure financial creditworthiness, a few of China's tech giants have created social credit-like systems of their own. Yet the relationship between these private initiatives and governmental scheme remains ambiguous and ambivalent. The concluding section will summarize the fundamental elements of the SCS as it stands, and identify the dimensions of potential transformation that may be used to guide future research.

I. Historical And Intellectual Roots

At the macro-level, the context in which the concept of social credit evolved is perhaps best characterized as one of the repeated efforts at building an effective, powerful and prosperous state. The term was mentioned first in the Nineties, in the context of the market-economic reforms that had started under the leadership of Deng Xiao-ping. These reforms themselves were the latest iteration in a series of attempts that had begun in the mid-19th Century, often abortive, to modernize China's state and society.

Early generations of reformers saw law as a key element of these reforms, exploring constitutional reform during the late Empire, and importing German and Japanese elements of civil codification. Yet successive generations of leaders were unable to establish stable domestic governance across the entire Chinese territory, and protect it from foreign intrusion. Consequently, law moved to the background in the overall picture of China's political transformation, replaced by hard-nosed focus on the acquisition and maintenance of power, often through military means. The first three decades of Communist Party rule were characterized by legal nihilism and continued turmoil. Law only regained a meaningful role in Chinese governance after the death of Mao, and China's entire legal system had to be rebuilt from the ground up.

This long period of neglect meant that many of the substantive and procedural developments that occurred in legal systems around the world throughout the 20th Century largely passed China by. The judicialization of constitutional protections and the introduction of human rights-based practices in Western countries, which occurred particularly after the Second World War, never gained a foothold in China.

While discussions about fundamental rights and the role of the state did take place in intellectual circles, China's Leninist governance system prioritizes the flexibility and discretion of its vanguard party. The 2014 4th Plenum clearly affirmed Party leadership over the legal system, while the doctrine of the 'Three Supremes' (sange zhishang) requires the judiciary to first and foremost observe the supremacy of the Party's cause. At the same time, it also meant that once the decision to reinvigorate the legal system was taken, there were few extant indigenous resources the system could lean on.

The result is that legal reform became a syncretic process integrating selectively adopted ideas from Chinese political history and lessons learnt from foreign legal systems. Exactly the fact that law is not seen as an autonomous sphere, but one intimately connected with politics and governance, means those pursuing legal and institutional innovation have cast a wider net in terms of inspiration. The SCS combines a number of these strands. The most important are first, the notion that the State is not merely in charge of legal authority, but should also foster social morality; and second, a positivist view of social reality based on systems theory, which holds that society can be understood and engineered through a holistic, scientific approach, blurring boundary between state and society, public and private.

The State As Promoter Of Moral Virtue

The close linkage between morality and authority lies at the heart of China's political tradition. The fundamental notion of imperial legitimacy, the Mandate of Heaven, holds that power is bestowed by Heaven unto a just ruler, and will be withheld from an unjust one. For centuries, the only path to officialdom lay through an examination system based on a canon of Confucian texts, which posited virtue as the central element of governing the person, the family, the region and the empire. Education was a crucial element of that process, and a primary task of officials.

By the late empire, state-sponsored schools had come into being. In rural areas, semi-monthly lectures (xiangyue) were organized to propagate the Sacred Edict, a list of sixteen maxims covering Confucian morality in a condensed matter, as well as oral vernacular expositions, not dissimilar to the homily in Catholic tradition.

The CCP has inherited and carried forward this mantle of moral authority, through its ambition to create 'new Socialist citizens'. Even after the Cultural Revolution, the period of reform and openness (gaige kaifang) did not repudiate that goal, but recast it as an integral part of social management. The construction of a 'spiritual civilization' (jingshen wenming) would accompany the concomitant progress in material and economic conditions. Moreover, legal and moral authority are fused, where lawful and morally just conduct are coterminous. Illustratively, the 4th Plenum denoted 'governing the country by virtue' (yide zhiguo) as equal to 'governing the country by the law' (yifa zhiguo).

Law thus is a tool to cultivate subjects' moral sentiments and transform their worldview, in order to achieve social and cosmic harmony." (And in footnoted writer Patricia M.) Thornton's view, "successive generations of Chinese rulers also instrumentalized morality and normative authority as part of a state-building process that sought to redraw the boundaries between the centre and the localities, as well as between state and society, in pursuit of shifting 'socio-ethical agendas'. The central state would portray itself as morally superior to its local agents. It would reframe political conflicts (which) would be redefined as moral failings, to be remedied by the deployment of both cooptive and coercive measures.

Individuals or forces who did not submit to these central efforts would be expunged from the state's ambit. Enforcing these moral standards justified expansion of the state's capacity to monitor and discipline the conduct of local officials, and to penetrate grass-roots society. While Thornton analyzes a period between the late Empire and the early People's Republic, these techniques are reflected even in the current anti-corruption campaign under Xi Jinping.

The SCS fits squarely in this tradition. From the very beginning, the compliance problem that the SCS is intended to solve has been framed in moralistic terms. In 2001 already, the People's Daily called for the creation of corporate and individual credit dossiers, arguing that sincerity, being the root of morality, was indispensible in developing China's market economy.

SCS policy documents claim its objective is to stimulate 'sincerity' (chengxin) and 'trustworthiness' (yongxin). The Joint Punishment System, analyzed in detail (to follow), explicitly targets acts of 'untrustworthiness' (shixin). The SCS can also be seen as a response to a moral crisis in politics. It came to prominence during a time where the political initiative had moved from the centre to the localities, resulting in perceptions of weak central leadership and rampant local corruption.

To the extent that the SCS is also aimed to better check the performance of local administrations, it forms part of efforts started in the second half of the Hu Jintao administration and accelerated under Xi Jinping to centralize power, strengthen discipline and return the Party and its 'mission civilatrice' (civilizing mission) back to prominence.

Complex Systems Engineering As Basic Theoretical Approach For Social Intervention

Chinese political tradition has, for centuries, conceived of society as an organic whole, where harmony can be achieved if all its members conduct themselves as appropriate to their position in public and civil structures. Yet not until the consolidation of CCP rule would there be a comprehensive governing authority, capable of penetrating society and influencing the daily lives of citizens nationwide.

After the disaster of the Cultural Revolution, the question of how to apply that authority in pursuit of national development fostered a search for applicable intellectual frameworks that would guide the Deng leadership's more pragmatic, institutionalizing policies. Critical in this process were ideas about systems theory, derived from natural science and applied social context. Influenced by Western scholarship on cybernetics and systems theory, scholars such as Qian Xuesen and Song Jian worked closely with government to develop a conceptual framework for the adoption of system engineering techniques in governance. Particular regard was given to the role of information flows, not just towards and within government, but also as part of cybernetic feedback loops to create self-correcting responses in society.

These ideas also underpinned the 'Golden Project', a series of plans to develop information systems within about a dozen policy areas. In the area of social management, the 'Golden Shield' project deserves particular attention. This is a programme to create a national infrastructure within the police and internal security bureaucracy, which has rapidly become ever more potent in recent years, accruing better technological, analysis and management capabilities.

A corollary of the holistic, systems-based conceptualization of social reality is that its elements are primarily evaluated in terms of their potential function in achieving the objectives of the system. Party members, individual citizens, government officials, business, neighbourhood committees and social organizations are all supposed to contribute to the realization of social harmony and economic development. This, in turn, blurs the boundaries between public and private actors.

In contrast, Western legal systems, lacking the strong technological focus of Chinese Communist Party (CCP) ideology, tend to delineate the rights, obligations, entitlements and responsibilities of public and private actor through well-delineated categories of state and society. As (the previously mentioned) Thornton posits, this fluidity between (the two) was already one of the key characteristics of late imperial society rendering traditional state-society dichotomies invalid for the case of China.

Philip C.C. Huang (well-known professor of history and author) reaches a similar conclusion, conceptualizing a 'third realm' that intermediated between the central state and the grass roots. Key players in this third realm were the scholar-gentry elites, usually educated and privately wealthy individuals without official appointments in the bureaucracy who, often on a voluntary basis, were active in local governance, tax collection and education. The central state also sought to overcome its limited capacity by mobilizing its subjects into forms of collective self-governance, such as the 'baojia' system in the Ming and Qing dynasties.

The SCS embodies this logic as made possible by information technology. Its core function is to create a system whereby the compliance of individuals and businesses with laws and regulations is increasingly monitored, and the consequences of non-compliance subject to swift and efficient sanction. Within this process, the support of private parties is enlisted for both information capture and enforcement. In other words, the 'social' dimension of the SCS entails that members of society create the incentives for each other to act in the desired manner, without direct intervention of State actors.

II. Early Steps Towards A SCS

The notion of social credit first emerged in debates concerning the development of China's nascent market economy. Trust was identified as a critical element in supporting market transaction, and one that in China was sorely lacking. The first high-level political mention of the social credit system came in the Political Report that the outgoing Secretary General Jiang Zemin delivered at the 16th Party Congress in 2002. This called for the establishment of a social credit system, as part of a broader effort to deepen modernization of the market system.

Here already, the separation between two major elements of the SCS was visible: on the one hand, credit referred to financial creditworthiness, similar to FICO scores in the United States; on the other hand, it referred to a broader notion of trust and honest conduct in the marketplace.

The People's Bank of China and related institutions took some initial steps to regulate financial credit reporting. Building on the 'Bank Credit Registry and Consulting System', established in 1997, the People's Bank of China established a 'Credit Reference Centre' in 2006, which was the only national credit-scoring bureau. Banks and other financial entities were obliged to report on their client's creditworthiness, with supplementary, non-financial information being transmitted from courts, government departments, telecommunications companies and fiscal authorities. However, at that time, comparatively few Chinese citizens held bank accounts, and the majority of transactions were settled in cash, making it more difficult to provide adequate and accurate credit scores. By 2012, only 280 million citizens were reported to have a credit report.

It would, however, take five years before the first concrete policy and organizational measures were taken concerning broader social credit ideas. In April 2007, the State Council established an interministerial joint conference for the construction of the SCS, with a membership clearly reflecting the primary economic nature of the initiative as it stood then. Its remit was framed broadly: planning the construction, researching and drafting major policy measures, trouble-shooting and overseeing policy implementation.

An accompanying State Council policy documented more specific objectives. First, it required the creation of better credit information records in the market economy, with particular reference to tax compliance, contract implementation and product quality. Second, it demanded the creation of credit information systems, particularly for the financial sector. Third, it called for the development of credit service markets, with government departments playing a leading role through increasing transparency of date it held on credit subjects within their jurisdiction. By that time some departments had already started working on ways to exchange information.

While the initial efforts surrounding the SCS were primarily focused on market economic concerns, the linkage between credit and social management started being explored in local initiatives. In some cases, such as in Yichang, this meant the creation of honorary titles, such as 'credit towns' and 'credit communities' for localities with a 'good credit atmosphere'. Perhaps the best-reported example, however, is the county of Suining, in Jiangsu province", with its 2010 introduction "of a 'mass credit' (dazhong xinyong) programme, which measured and scored individual conduct" through a point system - the salient, but certainly briefer details, than Mr. Creemers offers, which we've already examined earlier in this book. And Mr. Creemers also goes into great detail about the objections that were voiced about the Suining version of the program, also examined earlier in this book!

And Mr. Creemers goes on to say, "Nonetheless, the Suining system already contained the embryonic forms of several elements of subsequent social credit initiatives: the notion of disproportional disincentives against rule-breaking, public naming and shaming of wrongdoers, and most importantly, the expansion of the credit mechanism outside of the market economic context, also encompassing compliance with administrative regulations and urban management rules.

Another local initiative that followed in the wake of the 2007 policy emerged from the province of Zhejiang and its capital, Hangzhou. Hangzhou had already established a 'Credit Hangzhou' coordination mechanism involving 69 government departments in 2002, while the provincial government issued regulations about the collection and publication of credit information concerning enterprises in 2005. The following year, Hangzhou published a social credit system development plan of the 11th Five-Year Plan cycle, followed by the provincial-level equivalent in 2007. Going much further than the central plan, the Zhejiang provincial government expanded the definition of credit from the market economy to also include the sincerity of civil servants. It also foreshadowed the construction of information management infrastructure that would be necessary to scale credit mechanisms at anything above small-town level.

At the heart of its plan lay the use of information sharing platforms, one for corporations and one for individuals. For the latter, a three-stage process was envisaged. In the first stage, experiments with basic information systems took place in the individual localities and departments. During the second stage, information would be broadly collected. One focus was on specific professions, ranging from chartered accountants and land value appraisers to medical professionals, journalists and tour guides. A second focus was compliance with taxation regulations, lending obligations, performance in individual judgments and payment of utility and social security fees. The third stage comprised better cross-regional information sharing, as well as exploring new forms of using the information collected.

At the central level as well, it was realized that credit-related mechanisms could be applied to more fields than merely the market economy, particularly in managing Party and state actors, as well as in social management. This evolution coincided with a rapid expansion of security, surveillance and social management structures, as well as a renewed political focus on spiritual and moral affairs. The increasing adoption of smartphones and social media led to a public sphere buzzing with political scandals and rumours, but also fraud and depictions of a perceived moral vacuum. Revelations about scandalous conduct by local Party officials not only became near-daily occurrences, but the speed at which information was disseminated online meant they rapidly gained visibility in a manner that propaganda authorities were largely powerless to prevent."

Mr. Creemers proceeds to provide examples of such "scandalous" political and social behaviors; and adds, "Food security scandals, such as the discovery of melamine in infant milk formula, further eroded trust in government institutions. In response, the leadership initiated a resurgence of attention for 'spiritual civilization construction', amongst others by dedicating the 6th Plenum of the 17th Party Congress in 2011 to culture and ideology. The Decision emanating from the plenum called for construction of a credit system to foster sincerity in society, not only in commercial affairs, but also in matters of social and political morality.

This policy shift greatly affected the conception of the social credit system. It would not only focus on trustworthiness (and creditworthiness) in the marketplace, but was seen as having an important role in transforming the overall governance strategies and tactics of the CCP. Consequently, the membership of the Interministerial Joint Conference was expanded: high profile Party bodies such as the Central Discipline Inspection Committee (the internal antic-corruption watchdog), the Central Political Legal Committee (which oversees internal security, including the judiciary and the police), the Central Propaganda Department and the Central Leading Group for Spiritual Civilization Construction joined the group, together with a number of their associated ministries. The Supreme People's Court and Supreme People's Protectorate were also added, indicating a growing role for the judiciary.

With the mandate of the 6th Plenum, this group started drafting a much more ambitious and wide-ranging social credit plan, which saw the light of day in the spring of 2014.

III. The Social Credit System After 2014

The 2014 Social Credit Plan

The 2014 'Planning Outline for the Construction of a Social Credit System' remains the most authoritative blueprint for subsequent SCS efforts, and represented a major advance in political thought on social credit at the national level. Building on previous local initiatives, such as the ones in Hangzhou and Zhejiang described earlier, the new plan combined the economic aspects of credit, both concerning financial creditworthiness and trust in the market, with the broader initiative to enhance social harmony and discipline government.

It (also) put forward a timetable until 2020 for the realization of five major objectives: creating a legal and regulatory framework for the SCS, building credit investigation and oversight, fostering a flourishing market built on credit services, and completing incentive and punishment mechanisms.

(And) it identified priority fields in four major policy areas. In government affairs, the SCS would increase transparency, enhance lawful administration, build trustworthiness for government actors, and display the government as a model of sincere conduct. In the market economy, social credit would enhance efficiency, trust and transparency across a range of sectors, ranging from finance to construction, food and e-commerce. In social services, the SCS would enhance trust in healthcare providers, strengthen management over particular professions and enhance scrutiny over online conduct. Lastly, the introduction of credit mechanisms would enable courts to more effectively implement judgments, enhance information sharing about parties in lawsuits and support norms for the legal profession.

Moreover, the 2014 Plan focused on the creation of the underlying information infrastructure that would be required for the system's successful rollout. It systematically provided for standardized means to record credit-related information in different sections of the administration, databases to store this information at the central and local levels, the establishment of credit reporting mechanisms to enable public access to the information, as well as information sharing processes in order to counter the siloing of data within the bureaucracy.

The major programme that this infrastructure would support is a system of rewards and punishments on the basis of blacklists and redlists (which record particularly conspicuous merit). These incentive mechanisms would not only be implemented through governmental means, but also through market mechanisms and self-regulatory regimes in particular sectors. The final sections of the document address the development of credit service markets, data and information protection, and specific guidelines for implementation.

The 2014 plan thus created a comprehensive roadmap that is gradually being implemented, containing substantive provisions, as well as measures to create the underlying technical, bureaucratic and financial support systems. It identified the major mechanisms that would be implemented, in particular the incentive and punishment systems that now form the major operational elements of the SCS. Interestingly, however, the document does not identify quantitative scoring as an evaluation method. Neither does it contain reference to the sort of correlative big data analytics that foreign observers have ascribed to the SCS.

The Joint Punishment System

The major programme outlined in the 2014 Plan was a system of rewards and punishments for sincere and untrustworthy conduct. The principle behind punishments was disproportional sanction, as summarized in the phrase, 'if trust is broken in one place, restrictions are imposed everywhere'. The programme is based on a blacklist system: identified miscreants are entered on a published list, which means they are blocked from specific activities.

The first area where this mechanism was implemented, and still the most wide-ranging one, is the punishment system for 'untrustworthy persons subject to enforcement' (shixin bei zhixing ren), which addresses non-performance of legally binding judgments. Subsequently, individual departments starting developing their own, more focused blacklists for their own policy areas.

The origins of this system lie in the 2012 revision of the Civil Litigation Law, which stipulated that, where individuals did not carry out legal obligations arising from a court judgment, courts could prohibit them from leaving the country, create an entry in their credit file and publish their names in news media. As this principle was worded rather vaguely, individual courts started implementing these rules in an inconsistent manner.

In order to systematize matters, the Supreme People's Court issued more detailed regulations in 2013 for a comprehensive blacklist system. These stipulate that anyone who is obliged and capable of carrying out a valid legal document, such as a court order or administrative decision, and fails to do so, will be entered on a blacklist. In principle, they will remain on that list for a period of two years, except in certain circumstances, where that period may be extended. If they perform the required obligation earlier, a court may decide to remove them from the list. The rules required the SPC to publish the name list through mass media and online.

Moreover, government departments, supervisory institutions, financial institutions, sectoral associations and credit agencies were required to extend penalties to those listed in areas including government procurement, bid tendering, administrative approvals, government subsidies, access to credit, market access and assessment of qualifications. Lastly, where state employees, People's Congress or Consultative Conference members, State-owned enterprises or public institutions were listed, additional political scrutiny applied.

Early in 2016, 45 Party bodies, government departments and judicial institutions, including the national Development and Reform Commission, the Supreme People's Court, the People's Bank of China, and the Chinese Youth League concluded a memorandum of understanding to further clarify their respective roles in what had now become known as the Joint Punishment System."

I think we get the idea – the Joint Punishment System is quite an extensive and highly-developed system – which's details can appear to be overwhelming, and beyond the scope of this book! Nevertheless, one can be quite certain this book will return to this subject again!

Mr. Creemers concludes this section with, "The blacklist systems have received criticism both inside and outside of China, addressing both the principle of the punishment system and reported instances where the system did not work as prescribed. Apart from concerns about privacy and the principle of disproportional punishment, news media and institutions such as Human Rights Watch identified cases where individuals who had been politically active had been listed without proper notification, and without apparent recourse to appeals procedures.

Various documents, including the 2016 Opinions, indicate that individuals must receive prior warning before entry on the blacklist, and have the right to appeal. Where they fulfilled their legal obligations, courts must remove their information from the blacklist system within three days, and all bodies that imposed restrictions must remove these promptly. A question requiring further research is the extent to which this is the consequence of teething troubles, incompetence or intent. The NDRC (National Development and Reform Commission), for its part, has recognized the necessity of this element of the system to work, in order to buttress its legitimacy as a whole, and identified it as a priority area for revision.

The Social Credit System And Information Technology

The SCS is a poster-child example of what the Chinese government sees as a process of informatization in governance. It uses information technology to transform the manner in which Chinese government authorities manage both state and society, by horizontal and vertical information sharing, overcoming the principle-agent problems and departmental protectionism that continues to plague China's governance architecture, and digitizing data hitherto contained only on paper. To ensure this is possible, the supporting technical infrastructure must ensure that subjects are identifiable, information about them can be collected, stored, processed, shared and used.

A first, fundamental requirement for the system is to ensure everyone subject to it can be identified. This happens at two levels: first, ensuring that there is a uniform filing system that allocated unique identifiers to discrete subjects, and second, disabling actors from acting anonymously.

For individuals, the choice of identifier was relatively simple. The 2003 Identity Card Law already mandated that identity cards would carry a number that was the unique, lifelong identifier for a particular person. In 2004, a new generation of identity cards came into being, which carried an 18-digit code, replacing the 15-digit identifier present on older identity documents. The 18-digit code combines information about the issuing local authority, date of birth and individual sequencing.

In 2013, when the SPC commenced the implementation of the joint punishment system, accompanying regulations clearly indicated that the identity card number should be used for the purposes of that system. The requirement to limit anonymous conduct is not new; it is the reason for the introduction of number plates on cars, for instance. However, the broader adoption of digital technology caused new challenges.

To counter ubiquitous anonymity in the digital environment, the leadership intensified efforts to introduce real-name registration requirements, amongst others for acquiring (mobile) telephones, using online account-based systems, and in social media. Furthermore, the Chinese state is expanding its biometric identification databases to further enable identification of individuals and connecting the identification with state-held records.

For corporations and other legal persons, the bureaucratic task was somewhat more complicated. Historically, each regulator had their own numbering system under which they would register businesses and organizations. Consequently, a business would have one registration number for a business licence, another for fiscal purposes, another for social security services and yet another for any special regulatory regimes they would fall under. This not only hampered effective integration of government information systems, it also created a considerable amount of red tape.

The initiative to integrate the major numbering systems was known first as 'three licences into one' (san zheng he yi) and comprised administrative registration, tax registration and organizational registration. It was expanded to 'five licences into one' (wu zheng he yi) by adding social security and statistics registration numbers. Under this integrated system, only 'one licence and one code' (yi zhao yi ma) would be required.

The new coding system was dubbed the 'uniform social credit code' (tongyi shehui xinyong daima) again consisting of an 18-digit code. These unique identifiers, combined with real-name registration systems for the digital environment, enable government to increasingly connect incoming data points to individuals and businesses. These data points mostly comprise administrative and financial information, but are increasingly supplemented by other sources, such as the facial recognition cameras used in some of the local social credit projects. Also, the system is starting to use information originating from the private sector: ride-sharing service Didi Chuxing, for instance, is providing information on the number of black-listed passengers it carries.

The second step is the creation of databases where information from different sources can be appended to unique identifiers. Local governments had already established such websites prior to 2014, and formulated catalogues for information to be shared with the platform. The 2015 Shanghai catalogue, for instance, includes information from 99 work units, including 46 municipal administrative bodies, 17 district-level governments" and many more!

"In June 2015, the NDRC and the State Information Centre jointly inaugurated the 'Credit China' platform, designed in collaboration with Baidu. The objective of this website, and the underlying information platform it supports, is to concentrate all credit-related information members of the Interministerial Joint Conference, as well as governments at the local level, hold about individuals and corporate actors. Much of this information is also made publicly available, making the website itself one of the incentives in the SCS.

The final step in the process is processing and using the stored information in furtherance of social management objectives. The development of information technology has increasingly provided the storage, communication and computational capabilities not just to collect and share data, but also to process and analyse it to generate actionable insights.

Perhaps the best-known example of this is correlational big data analysis, which sorts individuals into categories on the basis of probabilistic computations. Yet at this point in time, with the exception of the narrow scope of financial credit scoring as discussed below, there seems to be little algorithmic processing of data. As far as public documents indicate, anyone's social credit status will only be influenced by the history of their own conduct to the extent that it is covered through the SCS's remit. Technological analysis is used, however, to make mass information more manageable, accessible or technologically presentable. For instance, the Big Data Key Scrutiny function within the blacklist system is intended to automatically flag individuals appearing on multiple lists. Similarly, the credit reports in the Honest Shanghai app reflect an integration of data from the existing credit databases.

IV. Private Social Credit Systems

Not only the Chinese government has occupied itself with social credit. Some of China's private tech businesses have done so well, spurred by the PBoC initiative to foster the development of a personal credit rating system akin to the FICO score system prevalent in the United States. In early 2015, the PBoC selected eight companies to begin 'preliminary work' (zhunbei gongzuo) for the establishment of formal credit reporting system, and gave them six months to do so.

Perhaps the best known of these systems is Sesame Credit, developed by Ant Financial Group, an affiliate of the E-commerce behemoth Alibaba." (Earlier in this book, we were already introduced to Sesame Credit.) Mr. Creemers continues, "Sesame Credit combines elements of a traditional credit scoring system with components of a loyalty scheme. It calculates a score between 350 points and 950 points based on the data in five major categories: 1) credit history, or records of past credit repayments; 2) behavioural trends, referring to someone's conduct when making purchases, processing payment, settling accounts and managing their finances; 3) ability to honour agreements, meaning having stable economic revenue and personal assets; 4) personal information, referring to the amount of verifiable and reliable information about themselves a member provides; and 5) social relationships, referring to the extent to which one interacts with good friends and behaves in a friendly manner on the platform. They respectively amount for 35%, 25%, 20%, 15% and 5% of the score, although the specific scoring algorithms remain confidential. Also, the platform gives little information on which specific actions would alter one's score, and to what extent.

While Sesame Credit remains an opt-in function in the broader Alibaba platform, this vagueness has raised concerns about the considerations that might be part of the scoring process, and to what extent they can inform policy that might one day be taken over by government. Although Ant later denied this, it had already fuelled foreign concerns about Sesame's alleged invasiveness and propensity for behavioural control.

Outside of its usefulness as a portable credit score, Sesame solved several problems that Alibaba faced in the development of its e-commerce business. The most important one of these concerned payment and creditworthiness. China was, at that time, still a largely cash-based economy, where few individuals held credit cards. Alibaba's model as an intermediary for purchasers and sellers required it to be able to facilitate payment. Without external broad-based providers, Alibaba decided to set up a mobile payment system of its own, which became known as Alipay. This, in turn, required Alibaba to be able to assess customers' financial creditworthiness. In the absence of a recorded financial history, they turned towards other useful proxies.

Second, Alibaba's business model depends on its ability to present itself as a trusted intermediary brokering between buyers and sellers who do not know each other. Sesame Credit was seen as a tool that could support this trust-building process. It is now also used outside the immediate financial context on the Alibaba platform. (On its dating service Baihe, for instance, hopeful singles often post their Sesame Credit scores in the hope that it will raise their attraction.)

As the adoption and the profile of Sesame Credit has grown, Ant Financial has increasingly expanded external partnerships, leveraging the trust infrastructure they created to facilitate linkages between consumers and other parties." And Mr. Creemers provides some examples of benefits consumers can receive from high Sesame Credit scores.

Mr. Creemers continues, "This raises the question to what extent Sesame collaborates with government, particularly on the government credit system. Popular news media have regularly conflated the two. However, at the time of writing, there is no hard evidence for this claim. Sesame's General manager, Hu Tao, wrote a letter to the Financial Times arguing the company anonymised and encrypted all user data before analysis, (and) gave users ample control over the extent to which their information was shared. Hu denied allegations both that Sesame was contracted to execute the government social credit system, and that it shared user data and scores with the government without users' prior consent.

At the same time, Alibaba is one of the private actors collaborating with the implementation of the blacklist scheme, disabling luxury purchases on its Taobao and Tmall platforms for designated individuals. Moreover, privacy seems to (have) become an increasing concern for users. In early 2018, Alipay introduced an annual reporting feature where users, by default, gave permission to access their Sesame scores. This led to an outcry on social media, a rapid reversal by Alipay, and a strongly worded apology.

From the point of view of the PBoC, which sought to develop the credit scoring industry, systems developed by Alibaba and other businesses involved were not successful. In fact, Tencent's version of a credit system was ordered shut down a day after it went into wider application. A first major problem the bank identified in its pursuit of both expanded domestic consumption and better financial risk control was that the eight businesses had developed their credit arms to support their core commercial, financial and insurance businesses, leading to conflicts of interest. There were also concerns about the accuracy of some of the data generated by the private scoring systems, often due to the fact that they could only capture credit data from their own customer bases and business activities.

Consequently, the PBoC decided not to extend the eight licences. A solution was found when the eight companies, together with the National Internet Finance Association (NIFA), jointly established a united credit scoring bureau, named Baihang. NIFA is a sectoral intermediary organization established in 2015, which falls under the administrative leadership of the PBoC." Footnote to NIFA: 'About NIFA.' NIFA. Online: http:// www.nifa.org.en/nifaen/ 2955866/2955892/index.html

And Mr. Creemers concludes this section with: "As such, and given NIFA holds a 36% stake in Baihang, PBoC control over tech-based scoring initiatives remains assured.

Conclusion

As it stands today, it is mistaken to conceive the Social Credit System as a single, integrated entity. Instead, the term covers an entire ecology of fragmented initiatives that share a basic set of objectives, operational frameworks and policy language. From the government's perspective, the two prime objectives are improving legal and regulatory compliance, which is the major purpose of the punishment systems, and developing the financial services industry.

For the private sector, this created opportunities to develop their own scoring systems, which combine the functions of user ratings on platforms and a loyalty scheme. While the concept of social credit originated as a means to remedy a perceived lack of trust in the marketplace; its purposes now also include combating benefit fraud, incentivizing domestic consumption and the development of new economic activities as part of a broader strategy to rebalance China's economic development process, lubricating the cogs of consumer commerce by inducing individuals, particularly the unbanked and underbanked, into a system where they can become trusted traders through verification and assessment by a reliable third party, harmonizing social conduct, and perhaps most importantly, devising new ways to discipline government actors.

It may thus be one example of what Jesper Schlaeger, Associate Professor at Sichuan University School of Public Administration, calls the 'battering ram', the use of information technologies to knock down the protective walls that subordinate government departments have erected to protect them from the scrutiny of their administrative superiors. At the same time, for the private businesses operating their own credit system, it has become a useful tool to reward loyal customers and render their platforms more attractive than those of competitors.

The SCS blurs the line between state and non-state actors. On the one hand, the blacklist mechanisms in the SCS amplify traditional law enforcement tools, vesting the norms to be enforced through the system in existing laws and regulations. With regard to financial scoring, however, the cash-based nature of China's economy meant developing a credit economy that required the use of non-financial proxy categories to substitute for a well-measured creditworthiness record.

In view of the conflicting statements by private businesses about their data collection and processing practices, the question of the extent to which they take the enforcement of social norms into consideration in this process is an open one, pending future research. However, the notion of private enforcement of social norms through credit reports itself is a promising topic for comparative research.

Early forms of credit reporting in the United States, such as the progenitors of today's Equifax, were explicit about their goal to impose 'discipline' on citizens. In this pursuit, credit investigators would include elements ranging from the stability of a s subject's marriage, their college grades, racial and gender prejudices, and the McCarthyite biases of the 1950s. Not until the Fair Credit Reporting Act of the 1970s would rights to personal data, limitations to information sharing and anti-discrimination requirements become part of federal law. The extent to which 'data justice' exists in today's economy remains a question worth asking.

The broader question remains whether the SCS is, or has the potential to become, the Orwellian nightmare many fear it to be: an omniscient machine hovering (sucking) up the massive amounts of data individuals generate as they plod through their lives, and processing it to deliver a quantified score that creates an ideological and consumerist straightjacket for every Chinese citizen.

Undoubtedly, Party ideology still fundamentally believes in social engineering on the basis of system science, on the malleability and transformability of the individual, and a rather maximalist approach to social intervention that sees the reading of the SCS as an attractive vision. Not only the SCS plan, but also national big data and artificial intelligence strategies explicitly intend the expanded use of automated, data-based systems for social control.

Leading Party media call for the use of these systems for informing, policymaking, automating internal government discipline, forecasting economic and social trends, and creating a situation in which 'government prepares the stage, society sings the harmony'. The underlying creation of information technologies that ensure more effective ways of 'seeing the state' indicates a commitment towards radical transparency: information on subjects' trustworthiness is to be made publicly available, and in some circumstances even actively broadcast. Similarly, information about the conduct of bureaucratic departments and, in some cases, their officials, as well as the compliance record of businesses, is to be made available.

Nevertheless, at present, the SCS remains a rather crude tool for social sorting. To a certain degree, this is perhaps due to the fact that the Chinese government does not see the need to control the conduct of its citizens through surreptitious or invisible means. Social control techniques prevalent in Western liberal democracies, such as gamification or nudging, are supposed to be largely unnoticeable: individuals are steered through the exploitation of inherent biases and unconscious decision-making strategies.

The SCS on the other hand does not hide its paternalism under a bushel: it is part of an openly declared and widely propagated effort to instill civic virtue, and conjoined with propaganda campaigns to raise individuals' consciousness about their actions.

More specifically, in order to assess whether and how the 'Orwellian' transformation is actually taking place, shifts (in) five dimensions will be useful in guiding future research. The first dimension concerns whether SCS data originates from government or private sources. At the present time, nearly all data on which decisions in the punishment systems are generated by government departments and recognized regulatory authorities. The information that informs financial credit scoring does also originate from the private sector, but is currently only used within this narrow scope.

The second dimension entails the nature of the rating system itself; whether it is binary or a more sophisticated ranking mechanism. The SCS punishment systems currently are clearly binary: one is either on or off the blacklist. The major central planning documents do not mention quantified scoring. In contrast, Sesame Credit, as well as the abortive Suining experiment and the ongoing Rongcheng trial, are examples of systems with a more fine-grained spectrum of outcomes based on a quantified assessment.

A third dimension consists of the nature of decision-making processes, whether judgments and scores are predominantly based on human assessments, programmed algorithms or self-changing deep learning applications over which humans have no full control. This is of particular importance when the SCS is to be used as a tool for normative control: if individuals are to comply with the rules and norms the SCS is built to support, these expectations should be transparent. Simply put, individuals need to know the benchmarks for optimizing their behavior. If automated decision systems do not enable this transparency, their role in social control may thus be limited.

A fourth dimension is the temporal orientation of judgments. At present, both the public and private scoring systems are past-oriented: they evaluate and rank individuals' previous conduct and append consequences in the present. A future-oriented system would act in a probabilistic manner, delineating scopes for actions based on individuals' expected or likely conduct in the future.

A fifth, connected dimension is whether decisions are made on an individual or collective basis. At present, the SCS only takes into account individual conduct; there is no statistical assessment on where this conduct falls in the distribution of the overall population. It may be the case that the private and financial credit systems do take into account how individuals compare to broader classes, but again, the coverage of these systems is comparatively narrow.

Future research on these developments also needs (to take) into account potential obstacles. The Party-State also faces no meaningful legal constraints against its actions per se. However, while Chinese government can do anything, it can't do everything. In particular, there are three categories of challenges that must be negotiated. The first one is external rejection. While it is not always easy for Chinese citizens to oppose particular policies, there is no shortage of examples where central and local government reconsidered or reversed decisions after popular unrest. Within the ambit of the SCS itself, the response to the abortive Suining trial demonstrates the difficulty of implementing a policy that is largely rejected by the citizenry. More recently, the government's response to increasing concerns about user privacy on the dominant online platforms Tencent and Alibaba, by shutting down the former's social credit trial and reprimanding the latter, further underscores the need to ensure citizens are, at least for the most part, on board with the programme."

And at this point, there's a strong need to interject: the scarcity of examples of effective resistance is startling and highly disquieting! That may be considered a more Western-oriented reaction, but in terms of humanity, it has to be a frightened one – considering that we're talking about near-monoliths in action, with artificial intelligence being a strong factor in decision-making! The implications for the human populations of states living under such regimes are immense; and incredibly threatening, considering that it is people that are at the head of these monoliths – people who unfortunately tend to act for people's reasons and motivations, in their nearly unchecked drive for power and control over other people – over their own; and often, over others not already under their effective control!

Mr. Creemers continues, "The second one" (category of challenges that must be negotiated) "is conflict between the various bureaucracies and actors that constitute the SCS. These tensions can be vertical, where the SCS is partly intended to be a tool to instill discipline over, and reduce the often-abused discretion of, the very same local governments on which the central system relies for information gathering, implementation and enforcement. The difficulties in integrating the various departmental punishment schemes further indicate the difficulty of coordinating large, cross-bureaucratic programmes in the Chinese context. The relationship between public and private actors is sometimes uneasy as well: government departments often consider corporate data gathering processes with a mixture of envy and concern.

The third category concerns enabling the system to work at a technical level. First, the quality of data going into the system itself needs to be guaranteed, otherwise the reliability of any of its outcomes is inevitably compromised. A particular problem will arise when individuals try to game the system by maximizing particular measured proxies. Compatibility and interoperability needs to be ensured between data storage formats and systems of central and local, public and private actors. Subsequently, the data needs to be processed and interpreted in a way that ensures the construction of meaning from the data results in useful information and legitimate decisions.

These three categories of constraints, external dissent, internal fragmentation, and difficulties in constructing underlying governmental architectures are, of course, not new to any observer of Chinese law and governance. They constitute some of the most fundamental pathologies at the heart of the Chinese polity. To a considerable degree, the SCS is based on the techno-optimist belief that automation might enable the state to transcend them. Yet ironically, they may well infect these very efforts too.

Lastly, future analysis of the SCS would do well to study its relationship with other social management projects. In functional terms, the SCS is currently relatively limited to market supervision and, to a certain degree, internal oversight. It is housed within a section of the bureaucracy that is less involved with politically salient and sensitive issues, and does not seem to include questions of crime, dissent and subversion. Rather, these are the province of a domestic security apparatus run entirely within the Ministry of Public Security and its associated entities. Here, we do find a large bureaucracy aimed at forecasting trends and informing pre-emptive decision-making, leveraging big data approaches as part of a ceaselessly intensifying risk-management and stabilization preservation effort.

In other words, the SCS should not be understood as a comprehensive governance tool, but as only one technology-empowered means of governance among many. Sometimes, these may learn from or build on each other, but analysis must also identify where they are distinct. Ideas, objectives, approaches, means and strategies for social control in China may emerge from a unified political context, but the complexities of organization and other intervening variables fragment them as much as they do the rest of China's political-legal landscape."

This is quite a presentation from Mr. Creemers; and one has to wonder how much of what he has to say reflects a certain naïveté of perhaps the outsider-looking-in; or rather a truly amazing, and perhaps scary, accuracy about, and insight into, the phenomenon that is Chinese Social Credit System?! We have a lot more information still to be presented that hopefully will help us better "rate" Mr. Creemers' personal and highly foot-noted understanding and insights into the SCS.

Continuing on, from this extensive examination of the writings of Mr. Creemers, what follows is a matter of delving further into the story behind the founding of the modern-day Chinese Social Credit System. "A Pioneer Of China's Credit System", written by Martin Li and published in the Shenzen Daily on September 14, 2012, tells the story of Huang Wenyun, as well as other important figures, in the founding of the modern-day Chinese Social Credit System.

I find it to be an interesting story, although I haven't come across other mentions of Ms. Huang that would more specifically corroborate many of the details of this story; nor, for that matter, have I seen any stories that might discredit its claims, about the important role Huang Wenyun played in this very significant development!

Mr. Li begins, "As the owner of a small electronics company, she may not be considered a player by Shenzhen's high-flying businesspeople, but Huang Wenyun is a big name in China's credit field. She is a pioneer of the country's credit system and has dedicated the past 12 years to developing the system.

Ten years ago, she funded a research team to examine the credit systems of the United States and Europe and wrote four letters to Zhu Rongji, then premier of China. These efforts led to a move to develop the country's credit system six years earlier than originally scheduled.

Aged 55, Huang is currently busy writing detailed suggestions on the country's credit management system.

'When they are completed, I will send them to the (incumbent) premier for reference,' said Huang.

Victim Of Counterfeiting

Huang came to Shenzhen in 1985 from her hometown in Wuxi, Jiangsu Province. The 28-year-old came to do foreign trade with her business partner. Seven years later, she established a company that specialized in toys that had educational value.

After devoting much time and money to developing her products, Huang's business became hugely profitable.

However, she soon met with misfortune. One of her products, a toy that was expected to achieve market sales of 10 million yuan (US$1.6 million), was counterfeited and sold across the city.

'I recovered less than half of what I had spent on the development and promotion of the toy,' Huang recalled.

Huang's suffering was exacerbated by the fact that the country's credit system was undeveloped.

On a visit to the United States in 1999, Huang was impressed by Americans' emphasis on credit construction. 'Americans take credit very seriously, where a powerful credit system covers loans, property insurance, medical insurance, endowment insurance and reemployment. A person may not be able to find a job if he or she has a bad credit rating,' said Huang.

Four Letters To Premier

Realizing the importance of a credit system, Huang wrote a letter at the end of July 1999 to then premier, Zhu Rongji, proposing the construction of a personal credit management system. 'As a conscientious Chinese citizen, I have been involved in business for many years and have a deep understanding of fairness and honesty in business. Completion of a fair credit system will play an important role in the development of the country's industrial circles,' Huang said in the letter.

Nowadays, it is easy for banks to check people's credit record in a credit information system when considering a loan. However, few people in China understood the importance of credit 12 years ago.

Huang's letter caught Zhu's attention, who transferred the letter to the then deputy head of the central bank – the People's Bank of China, Shang Fulin, and requested that action be taken.

On July 1, 2000, China's first personal credit information system opened in Shanghai, through which people's credit record could be checked. 'I didn't expect Premier Zhu to give such a quick response,' recalled Huang.

Huang was encouraged to provide professional support to the construction of the country's credit system.

She spent 300,000 yuan to cooperate with the Institute of World Economics & Politics of the Chinese Academy of Scial Sciences to set up a special research team in 1999, which involved Lin Junyue and Gao Lu, two young scholars who had studied in the United States and Europe respectively." (Note: remember the name Lin Junyue – there is no doubt that he was instrumental in the development of the modern-day Chinese Social Credit System! More on him will immediately follow this story.)

Mr. Li continues, "Huang funded and sent Lin and Gao to study credit management in the United States and Europe.

The resulting report was titled 'How To Build China's Social Credit Management System,' and was submitted by Huang to Zhu in January 2000.

Zhu soon summoned 10 related ministries to a meeting, discussing the issue.

Huang continued to visit domestic cities and summarized the problems hampering the development of the country's credit system. For the third time, Huang wrote a letter to Zhu in April 2002, which was followed by a meeting of 12 ministries.

Buoyed by her success, Huang funded the writing and publication of two books on social credit systems, which helped further pioneer the country's own system.

Influenced by Huang, the Ministry of Education in 2002 approved Shanghai University of Finance and Economics and Renmin University of China to open credit management courses to postgraduates. Now, there are more than 20 domestic universities that offer majors in credit management. In her fourth letter to Zhu, Huang mentioned high-tech crimes and proposed the construction of a State information security system to protect information.

At the end of each of Huang's four letters to Zhu Rongji, then China's premier, she identified herself as 'Huang Wenyun, a Shanghai citizen.'

No Regrets

Huang's devotion to helping develop the country's credit system has left her business sluggish. She has lost orders to competitors and seen a reduction in her country's market share. 'I don't regret the damage done to my business, because we all must make sacrifices to pursue our goals,' said Huang.

'My father used to be head of a factory in Shanghai. He was dedicated to his job and even refused to see a doctor when he was ill. He died of cancer. His dedication touched me. Each person should assume responsibility to make his or her contribution to society,' said Huang.

'It is satisfying to use one's abilities to do good,' said Huang.

Persevering

Huang is continuing her work on helping to develop the country's credit system. She is currently focusing on the incomplete regulation of the credit system. The system still lacks a unified standard and connection rules.

She is thinking about the framework of a national credit management system. 'Once I come up with detailed suggestions, I will write and send them to the (incumbent) premier for reference,' said Huang.

'The preservation of a market economy requires a spirit of trust. Credit is very important to building this trust. China has to build its credit system to develop a market economy. So my work matters,' said Huang.

Huang has come in for much praise from illustrious people. 'Huang is a true pioneer,' said (the important) Lin Junyue, who is deputy head of China Market Credit Management Association. Jiang Shaoli, who is deputy head of Shenzhen Xintu Internet Technology Co. Ltd, said Huang has a 'credit complex,' which explains her dedication to the cause. 'Huang has turned down offers of consultancy roles from many companies, but she offered free consultation to our company because it is located in Shenzhen,' said Jiang.

And Mr. Li ends by noting that "Jiang's company is the only domestic company engaged in personal professional credit management." And I'm sure that's changed in the intervening years, along with so many other things about China's developing Social Credit System!

Now, for a very significant – perhaps the most important perspective, on the early-stage development of the modern-day Chinese Social Credit System, we'll be examining Lin Junyue's in-depth views on the experiment. His viewpoint is so critical because he is credited with being one of the most important co-developers of the system itself; and the comprehensive article titled, "Retrospect: 1999-2009 Achievements In Social Credit System Construction Of China", appearing in the BIIA (Business Information Industry Association, a Not-For-Profit Hong Kong Organization) Newsletter February 2010 issue, (and still available on the biia.com website), is an important statement about the development of the system in his own highly-detailed words; as a direct participant, rather than by onlookers, knowledgeable and otherwise!

This document written by Lin Junyue, Vice Chairman, the Academic Committee of China Marketing Association and the Chairman of its branch of Market Credit Academic council; Chairman of the Academic Committee of Credit Management Professionals, Occupation Skill Testing Authority, of Ministry of Human Resources and Social Security of China, begins with the Abstract.

"Abstract: the social credit system, serving as a framework on which the government, enterprise and consumer credit systems are built, is a fundamental tool of putting in order the chronic chaos in the economic operation as well as a safety guarantee for the introduction of credit transaction and credit instruments in the market. Since it first put forward the concept of social credit system and its design framework in 1999, in the past ten years China has carved out a new path of constructing an effective credit reporting system through which China obtained lots of applicable experience and avoided certain unsuccessful steps experienced by some developing countries and has made a significant progress. The present paper introduces the theoretical pattern of China's construction of its social credit system and summarizes nine major achievements of this endeavor. It also makes a brief analysis on trend of social credit system construction that is regarded now as a national policy in China and highlights a number of aspects where more efforts are required for this purpose."

d the paper continues:

"I. Social Credit System And Its Operation Theory

As the foundation of the market economy, the social credit system ensures the success of all types of transactions on credit basis. The social credit system (SCS) of China, a creature of the age, emerged in response to the need for the in-depth development of China's market economy. It has painted a brilliant chapter in the spectacular book of the country's reform and opening-up to the outside world. In view of the global financial crisis, it seems that China has occupied a favorable position in this 'earthshaking change unprecedented in three thousand years'.

As for if China can avail itself of this momentum to advance its development toward a splendid future, its social credit system will play a decisive role. This year marks the tenth anniversary of the putting forward of the theory of social credit system with basic concepts and a framework design, and it is of especially great significance now to give a review of China's construction of this system.

The concept of social credit system was first put forward in August, 1999, when Zhu Rongji, the then premier of the State Council, made comments and instructions on a 'letter from ordinary people' – footnoted with: 'in the middle of August, 1999, Huang Wenyun, a woman entrepreneur from Shenzhen, wrote to Premier Zhu Rongji asking to improve the credit environment in the market, leading to the investigation and research on establishing a social credit system.' And Mr. Lin continues, "…thus unveiling the prelude of the research of social credit system in China.

In October, 1999, a research project titled 'Toward the Establishment of a National Credit Management System', the earliest research project concerning the establishment of a social credit system in China, was initiated in the Institute Of World Economics & Politics, Chinese Academy of Social Sciences. At the time, China was witnessing a steady rapid economic growth and embarking on the journey to an 'era of credit economy'. The constant expansion of the scale of credit transaction was requiring a corresponding market mechanism to support it. What's more, the chronic disorder of China's market economy was also anticipating a more effective and, fundamental in particular, regulating method.

The research group thought that the social credit system should have the nature of a large-scale infrastructure, that is, it should be able to ensure the information transparency of the transaction parties and, before carrying out a credit transaction, give the credit grantor access to the background information and payment records of the 'credit receiver' to have an accurate assessment of incumbent credit receiver's creditworthiness, thus solving the problem of information asymmetry between the two parties.

In function, the social credit system can not only blacklist the faith-breaking or delinquency parties but also reward the good-faith or low-risk parties. It punishes the delinquency or default party with economic means to foster a soft environment beneficial to the development of China's credit economy. As a large-scale infrastructure, the social credit system provides technical and enforcement support for the construction of enterprise and personal credit systems as well as for construction of a credit-keeping mechanism for the government. Technically, the social credit system in a narrow sense is the credit reporting system in a broad sense.

According to the definition by the research group, 'Social credit system is a new social mechanism that concerns a country's market regulation and aims to establish a market environment conductible for credit based transaction and facilitate the transition forms in a county toward credit transaction, viz, the healthy transition from transaction form dominated by cash payment to the one dominated by credit transaction. Therefore, the social credit system will establish a new set of market rules in China to ensure the large-scale and fair issuing of all kinds of commercial and financial credit instruments in the market as well as a high repayment rate favoring to credit grantors.'

As regards the specific approaches and solutions, the research group advised the central government to establish a 'credit reporting system' that serves both the market and the government supervision. When studying the practices of a number of developing Latin American and Asian countries, however, the research group found that their credit reporting systems were not efficient enough, and is some cases, had brought about some social problems and aggravated the government's fiscal burden.

In view of the complicated environment confronting China, such as the task of maintaining rapid economic growth, the disorder of the domestic market, and the fierce international competition, the credit reporting system to be established should not only get rid of a tortu(r)ous path of development, but it should identify a short-cut for China.

In order to avoid repeating the mistakes committed by other countries, the research group advised that to establish what they called a 'social credit system' in China, it should be implemented in a way in which the credit reporting system and the supplementary market environment are constructed together, (in order) to have the credit reporting system function in an efficient environment that provides such supports as legislation & regulation, college programs on credit management, introduction of practitioner certificate exam, upgrading of government of government supervision, establishment of professional associations, and establishment of credit systems within enterprises; thus providing the credit reporting system with well-trained professional, legitimate and transparent channels to collect information, and the market of credit reporting products and services, and constructing China's credit reporting system on a higher jumping-off point.

Under the guide of this concept, the research group designed the 'cognitive framework' of the basic functions of the social credit system to be divided into three parts: "1) trustworthiness morality propaganda, 2) financial and commercial credit instrument issuing, and 3) credit risk management: risk prevention of, risk transfer of, and risk control of market credit." And the research group "carried out in-depth study on the functioning of the system's credit rewarding and punishing mechanism."

And Mr. Lin continues, "In addition, the research group thought that the effect and impact of the social credit system should not be confined to the economic sphere, and it also holds major and far-reaching significance for restoring social moral(ity), and accelerating the formation of social capital in China. Therefore, on the basis of drawing on both the positive and negative experience of developed and developing countries, the research group put forward for the first time in China the proposition of establishing a 'national credit management system.'

Based on more than three years of research, the central government formally announced its decision to start-up the construction of social credit system in 2003. Drawing on previous researches, the government redefines the social credit system as follows: 'The social credit system is an effective social mechanism that, based on legislation and morality and with the credit institution at the core, records, exposes, disseminates and pre-warns against faith-breaking behaviors, (in order) to solve the information asymmetry problem in economic and social life, raise the cost for discredit/delinquency, punish faith-breaking behaviors and reward honesty and good faith; thus expanding the scale of credit based transaction in the market, maintaining the order of economic and social activities, and promoting healthy economic and social development.'

And Mr. Lin reports, "In 2006, the per capita GDP of China reached USD2042, with a number of cities where the per capita GDP topped USD6000. Some experts, citing pertaining economic theories, held that China had formally stepped on the stage of credit economy and that the volume of the credit economy would be approaching or exceeding 50% of the total volume of the economy. The year 2006, as a matter of fact, marked 'the beginning year of credit economy' in China.

For a long time, the social credit system has played a guardian role for credit transaction and its significance cannot be disputed. Research has found that there is a positive correlation between the scale of a country's credit economic activity, credit transaction and its GDP, with the correlation coefficient reaching 0.9199. According to a regression analysis of the economic development of U.S., Germany, Japan, France and Korea in the period between 1991 and 2001, for every increment of USD100 million of credit transaction, there would come about a GDP growth equivalent to USD23.53 million. The effective and secure application of credit instruments holds great significance for the improvement of a country's comprehensive strength.

Given that any credit instrument entails certain risk, the social credit system has provided the credit transactions in the market with technical measures and services of preventing, controlling and transferring credit risk, and has significantly improved the high repayment rate of credit transactions. In the past decade, the financial institutions have introduced many credit instruments in large scale, with 50% of all enterprises whose credit sales reached three quarters of their total sales. Without the protection of a sound credit system, this would be unimaginable.

With a fast-growing economy, it is of immense significance for China to establish its social credit system, and according to some experts, the system is as important as China's social security system. The establishment of the social credit system has the following significances:

1) Making credit transaction the main form of transaction in the market: The large-scale introduction of financial credit instruments have seen a large increase, and the scale of enterprises selling products on credit and their credit sales have increased by dozens of times.

2) Guaranteeing the high repayment rate of credit base transactions: The system has prevented, controlled and transferred credit risk, safeguarded the introduction of credit instruments, and improved the market's efficiency.

3) Providing a fundamental tool of rectifying the disorder in domestic market: The credit rewarding and punishing mechanism has the lasting function of regulating discreditable economic behaviors, and in particular, it can punish such behaviors in all levels and corners of the market and warn against such motivations.

4) Improving the government's supervisory capacity: The system upgraded the government's means in supervising the enterprises and improved its supervisory capacity.

5) Advancing the education of trustworthiness morality: In a sense, the construction of the social credit system is a campaign of promoting honesty, trust, morality and credit. In the campaign, rewarding the creditable behaviors and punishing the discreditable behaviors provide a powerful guide of values and help to form a more advanced culture and also indirectly change the people's life style.

6) Significantly accelerating the construction and improving the operating efficiency of the credit reporting system: The model of China's social credit system pursues efficiency of construction and efficiency of operation to catch up with or surpass the developed countries in the construction of credit reporting system.

II. Achievements Of China's Social Credit System Construction In This Decade

It has been ten years since China first put forward the concept and its running theory of social credit system. Having undergone four years of investigative preparation and six years of construction, China's construction of the social credit system has witnessed significant progress, despite the fact that its infrastructure construction is still in the preliminary stage and the system's operation is less than smooth. In retrospect, China has scored the following achievement in the construction of its social credit system:

A) A Chinese Model Of Social Credit System Has Been Formed

Since it put forward for the first time the concept of 'social credit system' in 1999, the Institute of World Economics & Politics under the Chinese Academy of Social Sciences has accomplished fruitful research results through extensive investigations and pilot explorations and has formed an increasingly clear theoretical framework. Meanwhile, it has also accumulated great practical experiences from different layers and perspectives.

Thanks to these efforts, a new model of constructing a credit reporting system has gradually taken shape in China. The credit reporting system as defined under the social credit system of China consists of two parts, namely a credit reporting service in the broad sense and a credit supervision system of the government. The broad-sense credit reporting system covers such industries as business credit reporting, consumer credit reporting, credit rating, debt collection, credit insurance, factoring, credit guarantee and marketing research.

The main reason why China endeavors to establish its own model of the social credit system is to avoid detours and improve the system's operation efficiency. China's 'model of social credit system' mainly has the following four characteristics:

1) Under the guide of the constantly improved theory of the social credit system, the construction of the broad-sense credit reporting system and that of its operating environment are integrated to achieve the best results. Unlike some Latin American countries which establish their credit reporting systems separately, China establishes its credit reporting system with a constant eye to building its social credit system on a more solid foundation.

2) The strengths of all sectors of society are mobilized to bring into full play the enthusiasm of all kinds of enterprises and all levels of government, thus forming a favorable 'all hands joining together' situation for building the social credit system and having the concepts of 'credit' and 'good faith' strike roots in people's minds. This has an important role to play in the moral restoration in China and enabling these concepts to become the mainstream of China's business culture. In other words, while establishing the credit rewarding and punishing mechanism, efforts are also taken to carry out credit education in the society in order to improve the moral standards of the people.

3) Endeavors in such aspects as infrastructure, human resources, legal regulation and moral education are carried out simultaneously to create a good external technical support and policy environment. And this also helps to create market demand for credit reporting products and services, improve the operation efficiency of the infrastructure of the social credit system, and lower the operation cost of the system.

4) Negative experiences of some countries are brought to our attention to prevent the arising of possible social problems in the course of the system's operation, and bring into full play the government's credit supervision by upgrading its supervision system and building the government capacity of supervising over enterprise credit; thus avoiding sluggish supervision as exposed by the flawed supervision of the United States over the credit rating and credit insurance industries in the sub-prime mortgage crisis.

The social credit system developed by China should be suitable for application in other developing countries and the experience it accumulated in the ten years of constructing the system can also be drawn upon by them, thus contributing to the world.

In the course of building 'the Chinese model of social credit system', the Academic Committee on Credit system with China Market Society (established in 2005 with Prof. Justin Lin elected as chairman, Lin Junyue elected as executive director, and Zhu Rongen and Wu Jingmei deputy directors at the first plenary session) has conducted a large amount of research work on the basic theories and technical matters as well as published more than twenty theoretical and technical monographs.

B) Great Strides Are Made In The Credit Reporting Industry

According to the definition in the national standard 'Credit – General Vocabulary', the broad-sense credit reporting industry covers nine sub-industries: business credit reporting, consumer credit reporting, credit rating, debt collection, credit insurance, factoring, marketing research, credit guarantee and credit management consulting.

In the recent ten years, except for the factoring and debt collection service, all other sub-industries have seen booming development. At present, the credit reporting industry has been able to provide the market with a moderately complete range of credit reporting products and services. It provides all kinds of credit grantors with comprehensive external technical supports of preventing, controlling and transferring credit risks and ensures the security of credit sales and the reliability of financial credit instruments. This has helped to significantly improve the success rate of credit transaction, accompanied by dozens of times increase of the introduction of credit instruments in the market and an increase of the number of enterprises confident to sell on credit.

A number of mainstream business credit reporting agencies, represented by such leading enterprises as Sinotrust, Huaxia D&B China, CIB, and Crediteyes, have been formed in the business credit reporting industry, which has been witnessing a growth of between 25% and 35% every year. In the year 2008 alone, the business credit reporting agencies issued more than 220,000 credit reports (exclusive of those provided by public agencies). In addition, the business credit information database has also seen rapid growth, and the online credit information service has become increasingly popular.

Since the 1990s, a number of leading enterprises in the credit rating industry have gradually taken shape, such as CCXI, Dagong Credit, Lianhe Ratings, YDPG, SBCR, and Pengyuan Credit Rating, and the business scope and professionalism have been constantly improving. With the rapid growth of credit rating institutions committed to serving government and industries, uniform credit rating institutions have also begun to emerge. In 2007 and 2008, in particular, the credit rating industry was especially thriving and the output value of the leading enterprises witnessed doubled growth. At present, some Chinese credit rating enterprises are even considering taking advantage of the opportunity brought by the financial crisis to enter the U.S. market.

In recent years, the consumer debt collection service has grown fivefold. Almost all commercial banks have commended (sent/transferred/sold?) the collection of the outstanding payment of their customers to third-party debt collection agencies. The monthly volume of debt collection commended by the grantor institutions and communication service providers has exceeded RMB one billion. In addition, with the significant growth of overseas debt collection business, some leading Chinese debt collection agencies are beginning to establish their overseas business networks and even considering opening overseas subsidiaries.

As regards China's export credit insurance business, the annual growth of its underwriting amount and premium has both averaged at nearly 70%, and the underwriting amount of internal trade has exceeded more than RMB 100 billion. In recent years, several foreign credit insurers, such as Euler & Hermes, Atradius Trade Credit Insurance Inc and Coface have entered the Chinese internal trade credit insurance market. Besides, leading Chinese insurers such as PICC&C and CPIC have also successively opened credit insurance services for internal trade. And thanks to the Chinese government's concern about the financial straits faced by small and medium-sized enterprise and its positive efforts in this regard, the credit guarantee sector has also witnessed rapid development.

C) A Fledging Public Credit Reporting System Has Been Put Into Use

China started to construct its public consumer credit reporting system in early 2004 and a national unified consumer credit information database was formally put into use in January 2006. At the time, it established credit records for more than 340 million consumers, including about 35 million with loan payment history. By the end of 2005, the database registered a consumer credit balance of RMB2.2 trillion, accounting for about 97.5% of the country's total consumer loan balance.

As of the end of 2008, the enterprise credit reporting system, initiated in 1997, had registered 14.47 million enterprises and other organizations, and the consumer credit reporting system had registered 640 million consumers, including 140 million with credit histories.

D) A Full Range Of National Credit Standards Have Been Promulgated

In the absence of a complete set of laws and regulations, the national standards assume special prominence. The designing and planning of the credit standardization framework was launched in 2004, and in the recent two years, the Standardization Administration of China (SAC) has promulgated a series of national standards concerning credit.

Since June 30, 2008, and through 2009, SAC has successively promulgated nine national credit standards covering:

1) Expression of enterprise's credit grade
2) Credit – general vocabulary
3) Rules for enterprise credit information collecting, processing and providing
4) Evaluation service specification for credit agency organization – Credit rating agency
5) Data item specification for enterprise credit
6) General rules of grading enterprise quality credit
7) Guidelines for standardization of credit
8) Credit evaluation norms for qualified suppliers
9) Classifying and coding of enterprise credit evaluation index system"

And Mr. Lin adds that there also is "pending implementation of more national credit standards." And says that, "In terms of both speed and scale of formulating standards for credit management and credit reporting, China is leading the world, giving a strong support to China's proposition to the International Standard Organization that a credit technical sub-committee be established.

E) Vigorously Increase Input
In Major Of Credit Management Of Higher Education

The major of Credit Management at China's universities, whose scale and level is unique throughout the world, has cultivated a great number of professionals of different levels in credit management and credit information.

Originated in 2002, the enrollment of China's undergraduate education for the major of Credit Management was first conducted in autumn by People's University of China, Shanghai University of Finance and Economics, and Capital University of Economics and Business. Over ten universities have set up the major of Credit Management in the past seven years.

In the past seven years, almost one thousand undergraduates majoring in Credit Management have graduated. These undergraduates, excluding those who continue to pursue their post-graduate degrees and (those) going abroad, have a good employment prospect and are in great demand in the human resources market. Some universities provide the graduates with employment opportunities by signing agreements with large-sized Chinese-funded enterprises, promising to provide them with graduates majoring in Credit Management.

From the employment trend of the graduates, we can conclude that the majority of them are taking on the jobs of management of credit risks in commercial banks and other financial institutions, a small number of them are working in state-owned enterprises or foreign-funded enterprises, and few of them devote themselves to the credit information services.

F) Preliminarily Perfect The System Of
National Vocational Qualification (License for Employment)
For Credit Management Professionals

In March 2005, the former Ministry of Labor and Social Security of China officially issued the occupation of 'credit management professionals', setting up a new occupation. In 2007, the occupation of credit management professional ... was listed into the Occupational Classification Canon (enlarged edition) of People's Republic of China authorized by the former Ministry of Labor and Social Security of China. The certificate of National Vocational Qualification for Credit Management Professionals is a 'business license' to managers for credit management and technicians for credit information services.

In January 2006, the Ministry of Labor and Social Security of China enacted the National Occupational Standards for Credit Management Professionals in which the 'occupation of credit management professionals' is defined as follows: professionals take on the tasks of credit risk management and credit information services. In the same year, the Ministry of Labor and Social Security of China set up 'National Occupation Skills Testing Authority Professional Committee of Professional Committee of Credit Management Division' (Note: direct quote from paper – not typo) to offer technical guidance and appointed China Market Credit Management Association to be in charge of the technical supports.

In October 2006, the government held the National Vocational Qualification Test for the first time. 2,392 people had taken part in the training for the Test for Credit Management Professional of the National Vocational Qualification Test by November 2008, among which 800 people had gotten the certificates of different levels. And initiatives have followed for improved training, and for developing the skills required for different kinds of posts in the fields of credit evaluation, credit analysis, debt management, credit investigation and researches in business.

G) Give An Impetus To The Development
   Of Urban And Regional Credit System

Since the central government established the pilot of credit system in Shanghai in 1999, many provinces or cities have gotten down to the (involved with) local credit systems, coming up with the slogans such as 'creating the city with sound credit' and 'rebuilding the credit for the city'. So far, over 20 provincial governments have established the special credit offices to promote the development of the local credit system. At present, the provinces such as Jiangsu, Hunan, Liaoning and Heilongjiang are actively promoting the development of regional credit system.

In accordance with the design theory of the social credit system and the political system of our country, the minimum unit suitable for establishing the independent credit system is the city. Therefore, many cities have established the credit systems or credibility systems. In recent years, many cities have strengthened their efforts to conduct the preliminary feasibility studies on the development of the urban credit system, which is even considered to be listed into the local development plans. The plans and researches conducted between the year 2003-2006 on development of the local credit system by some provinces and cities show that, among these cities, Wenzhou and Shantou are the first cities that established the urban credit system, while Shenzhen, Hangzhou and Anshan, the development of the credit systems of which have their unique features, have gained a great amount of experience. In terms of the development of the urban credit system in China, (it should be noted that) Shanghai focuses on that of the individuals while the majority of provinces and cities focus on that of the enterprises.

H) Vigorously Carrying Out The Enterprise Credit System

With the function of supporting the development of the credit systems of the enterprises, individuals and government, the social credit system has made progress in terms of supporting the development of the credit systems of the enterprises in the past ten years.

With the further development of the social credit system in China, the market credit information services is increasingly mature, the credit supervision system of the government is promptly upgrading, and personnel market for the major (in) credit management is also gradually taking shape. Thus, the external systems and environments for establishing the credit system of the enterprise have been formed. An increasing number of enterprises begin to adopt the method of credit sales in order to gain great market shares under the environment of credit economy. With the demand of perfecting the function of credit management of their own, more and more enterprises start to set up credit management department in charge of controlling the risks in credit sales.

Therefore, the external systems and environments for establishing the credit system of the enterprises have also been formed.

I/J) Establish And Play The Role Of The Credit Supervision System Of The Government

In China, the government departments with the function of supervision will respond quickly in establishing the credit supervision system as long as they are called on to do so by the Central Committee of the Communist Party of China and the State Council. The government departments can get substantial financial support from the Chinese government, a government with mighty power.

Since 2000, the supervision departments of the governments in some provinces and cities have begun to attempt to conduct the credit supervision. For example, the 'experiments' have been carried out by the administration for industry and commerce in Fuyang city, Zhejiang province and Beijing Administration for Industry and Commerce. In 2003, the central government officially announced the launch and development of the social credit system. The State Administration for Industry and Commerce took the initiative to establish the credit management system under the guidance of Wu Yi, the vice premier of our country at that time, and conducted four levels of supervision methods on the enterprises. At the present, the People's Bank, the State Administration of Taxation, Local Administration of Taxation, General Administration of Quality Supervision Inspection Quarantine of the People's Republic of China and General Administration of Customs of the People's Republic of China have established the credit supervision system in succession.

Such a large-scale development of the credit supervision system promoted by the Chinese government, which is unique throughout the world, upgrades the supervision systems of, and improves the level of supervision of, the government.

III) Expectations to The Development Of Social Credit System

Nowadays (2010), countries throughout the world are under the rather serious international financial crisis, which resulted from the structured finance of the American financial market, including the over-issuance and excessive investment of the credit derivatives; and reduced the whole world to the most difficult situation since the Great Depression in the last century.

From the source of this financial crisis, we can conclude that the subprime crisis of the U.S. is a 'credit tool' of the low-quality structured finance excessively issued by the bankers, who deviated from the technology of the financial innovations and code of ethics. The International Credit Rating Organization and the credit assurance organizations in the U.S., who played the jackal to the tiger in order to pursue the economic interests, together with the American government, who was negligent of the financial innovation and control of monetary speculation, led to the consequence that the financial institutions and credit rating organizations exploited the loophole of the credit system.

As a country that has been integrated into the world economy market, China is also involved (has also been brought) into this financial crisis, and (is) in the hardest times since the implementation of the policy of reform and opening up to the outside. In order to deal with the financial crisis, the central government put RMB4,000 billion Yuan to use for stimulating the economy recovery, formulated plans for rejuvenating ten industries, and issued over 30 supporting documents within this period.

The measures taken by the Chinese government are unprecedented, showing the great efforts of the government. There has been some signs of recovery of China's economy after several months of efforts. However, the economic data of the first two quarters of 2009 shows that no great progress has been made. It is undeniable that there are signs, but no assurance to the recovery of China's economy. We hope that the economic recovery of China can rebound in V-shaped, rather than the W-shaped economy of the U.S., which was described by Paul Kruger, a winner in Nobel Prize in economics, in the following way: 'it (the American economy) is sliding, slightly recovering and sliding deeper.'

In terms of 'how to make use of the RMB 4,000 billion Yuan for stimulating the economic recovery', the Chinese government came up with the strategies of 'maintaining the economic growth, expanding the domestic demand, and adjusting the structure' to cope with the crisis. Currently, the deficiencies in our economy are that the consumption contributes too less (too little) to the economic growth, the industrial structures are imbalanced, and social security system is incomplete.

Of course, the Chinese government, by taking advantage of reversed transmission of the pressure for easing monetary condition of the crisis, probably will make great determination to conduct the adjustments and promote the sustainable development in the future, at the expense of the current interest. However, this target is difficult to achieve, as the investment in the social security system and social credit system, which is inadequate in earlier years, can't make contributions to the expanding of the domestic demand. Thus, the target of 'maintaining the economic growth' has become the top priority. But the target of 'maintaining the economic growth' is becoming a 'competition for investment' and a great amount of capital is flowing into the industries with over production capacity.

With the market economy of China becoming more and more mature, we can find that the social credit system, a pillar to the modern market economy, and the social security system are of paramount importance. As time went on, we feel that this idea is not exaggerated under the environment of global crisis. From the phenomena mentioned above, we feel more deeply that it is a meaningful thing to commemorate the tenth anniversary of the idea and theoretical frame of the social credit system. If the social credit system is complete, it is able to play its role in getting rid of possible credit risks and making contributions in stimulating consumption. We greatly hope that the social credit system can play a greater role in economic recovery, especially in the aspect of expanding the domestic demand.

The global financial crisis caused by the subprime crisis sounded an alarm for our country. China will learn from the experience, quicken the development and perfect all the functions of the social credit system. In accordance with the joint conference of the State Council about the social credit system of China, we can expect that the development of the social credit system will be conducted in the following ways:

1) Chinese government will unswervingly promote the development of the social credit system and quicken the speed in development of the credit database of various kinds and the infrastructure facilities of the credit supervision system. The government authorities and the division of the work of the government sectors will be further specified.

2) Dramatic breakthroughs will be made in the relevant legislation work about the credit of the central government and great importance will be attached to the legislation work of other relevant laws.

3) The formulation of relevant standards about the credit will continue to be promoted and the popularization and application of the national standards will be vigorously strengthened. China will further interfere (participate) in the formulation of the relevant

international standards and carry out closer cooperation with the International Organization for Standardization. Meanwhile the conference about certification and approval to the credit information services and technicians with credit information will be held.

4) The research work of the credit management and technology about credit, will be further highlighted and importance will be further attached to the core technology by the credit agencies. The level of technology of the whole industry will be generally improved, specifically in the fields of Business Credit Reporting, Customer Credit Reporting, credit ratings, credit guarantee, credit insurance and credit management consulting, etc.

5) The research institutes, industrial groups and credit information services in China will learn from the experience of the development of the social credit system. Said experience, which may exert an impact on the international community, will probably spread to the other developing countries.

6) With the increasingly mature supervision to the credit information services by the government, the credit information services will develop in a standardized way, some of which will keep a robust growth. Moreover, the foreign exchanges of the credit information services will be highlighted and more foreign counterparts will run their business in China, which enables the Chinese-funded credit information services to establish branches abroad.

7) The scale of the universities setting up the courses of credit management will be further expanded. Each university setting up the major of credit management will specify the development direction of their majors, which can help change the situation (so that) all the majors about credit management flock together in the school of finance.

8) The new occupations in credit industry will emerge in our country. The new occupations for conducting 'credit analysis' for the credit rating industry and 'credit investigation' for the credit industry may emerge in succession apart from the occupation of 'credit management professionals' set for the credit managers of the enterprises.

9) The government and enterprises will pay more attention to the development of the credit system and the number of enterprises with credit management sectors will further increase.

In spite of the great achievements in the development of the social credit system, China only took the first step and still has a long way to go. The development work in some fields is still needed to be strengthened and deficiencies and potential troubles in design are needed to be tackled. China should make greater efforts in the development of the social credit system:

A) It's still a doubt that (there's still doubt about) whether the Chinese government can promote the development of credit information reporting services by taking advantage of its characteristic of swimming against the economic crisis. The financial crisis is a rare chance for the maturity and development of the credit information reporting services. We hope that the government can stipulate the policies promoting the development of the credit information services.

B) The planning work to the development of the social credit system of China has always been in a hysteretic (in flux, changing, changeable) state. There is no special plan for the development of the social credit system despite that the relevant research institutes have finished some subject studies.

C) The capital invested into the development of theory of credit economy and credit technology is so little that it is unable to meet the requirements of obtaining the core technology of the credit information services and the systematic study of the Credit Economics. At the tenth anniversary of the birth of the idea of the social credit system and its theoretical frame, China needs to review its past experience to form its own development mode and increase the capital for scientific research. At the National People's Congress and the Chinese People's Political Consultative Congress, the members of the CPPCC National Committee advised the government and relevant research departments to establish some special research institutions or suggested that the departments studying the economic security should conduct the long-term research on the establishment of the rules for credit economy and prevention of the credit risks, hoping that the government could accept their proposals.

D) The opening and sharing of the credit information has been a difficult problem for a long time. The key to solve the problem is to specify the responsibility of the government authorities and improve the mechanism. Besides, the policies aiming at the problems of economic security and information security also have to be made. Moreover, the dispute between the 'public mode' and 'private mode' existing in the development of the credit system should be specified by using relevant policies and solved in accordance with the laws.

E) The branches of the credit information services should be open to the public as quickly as possible, as the complete products and services are needed in the implementation of credit management in the whole process. Although the Ministry of Commerce vigorously advocates the debt collection industry and the factoring industry, a series of preparations in policies and supervision as well as the cooperation of other relevant government sections are also in need.

F) Although the credit information services are gradually growing up, some of which even have created several mainstream institutions, those top credit information services may become the targets that are merged by the foreign-invested companies. The introduction of the foreign investment causes continuous restructuring in this industry.

It is stressed that the credit information service is an industry swimming against the economic crisis, which can be proven by the development history of the credit information services in the developed countries. Therefore, the Chinese government can turn the bad things to a good one to the extent possible by taking good advantage of this financial crisis; while paying attention to the adjustment of the economic structure, the government will promote the development of the credit information as a 'watchdog' for preventing financial risks.

We should not forget that the main task of the development of the social credit system is to build a powerful credit system. Thus, the Chinese government may take measures to encourage the capital to be vigorously invested into the fields of the credit information services and the technical study about the control of credit risks.

If the government has greater ambition, it may consider making use of the advantage of the credit information services: swimming against the economic crisis, set up the core institutions to help them enter the international market and actively participate in the formulation of relevant international rules. Moreover, it's high time that the modes and experience of the development of the social credit system of China should be popularized to the whole world, which is beneficial to the formation of China's soft power.

In the 'changed situation' caused by the international financial crisis, China probably may have some advantages despite that it is unable to pay no attention to (ignore) other countries. The key issue is whether China can make good use of this golden chance offered by the formulation of the international economic/financial regulations on the basis of maintaining the tendency of the economic recovery, which can prevent China from being trapped in the 'law of jungle' and do good to the national rejuvenation. It is our country itself that determines whether we can have a bright future.

Wen Jiabao, the premier of our country, ever said that if a nation can't be far-sighted, it's hopeless. The Chinese people hope to see the scenes that the Chinese government is able to fully bring its exceptional intelligence and wisdom into play, resist the negative effects brought by the financial crisis and make the western countries realize the legitimacy of the Chinese economic system. In this way, the technology for controlling the credit risks of the social credit system of China and the beliefs of honesty and good morality supporting the system can make greater contributions to the social and economic development of countries throughout the world."

And I'll follow this long and substantive piece with a fairly short one – that looks at the Chinese social credit system in action from a still relatively early, and perhaps cautious, perspective. The article is titled "China's New Social Credit System", and subtitled, "Despite Hyped Concerns In The Foreign Press, Little Is Actually known About China's Plan To Rate Citizens And Firms." The article is written by Sara Hsu, and dated May 10, 2015; and posted on The Diplomat (https://thediplomat.com).

Ms. Hsu begins, "Last summer, China released an outline of its new social credit system, which would rate citizens and firms on financial, legal and civic terms. There has been much hoopla in recent Western media outlets about the system, with some viewing it as a return to the dang'an systems, which was highly opaque and inaccessible to the individuals and firms being rated. The interpretation of the new policy as an imposition of a 'Big Brother' type of invasive tracking system may be largely exaggerated, and how this understanding was arrived at is unclear.

The policy itself states that 'records of sincerity,' including reports on credit, legal violations, and performance will be kept, although the document, like most state documents is quite vague. The document is extensive," (as will be demonstrated in a very lengthy examination of this particular document shortly after this one!) "discussing credit in administrative areas, commercial activities, social behavior, and the judicial system. Individuals will hold identification cards associated with credit information, based on financial, industrial and commercial registration, taxes, and social security payments, and traffic violations, according to Xinhua. This leaves its implementation open to interpretation.

Already the policy has been implemented by China Customs to rate enterprises as 'Certified Enterprise,' the 'General Enterprise,' and the 'Discredited Enterprise,' based on compliance with anti-smuggling and other legal rules. The China Association of Construction Enterprise Management also announced its launch of an online credit system.

The social credit system includes financial scoring information, which has been lacking in China, to help individuals and institutions more easily obtain financing. The financial system currently relies on credit information history provided internally by banks or other financial institutions that obtain financial records from past transactions as well as some basic financial information about individuals. While credit ratings for some institutions are available through companies like Dagong Global Credit Rating, a widespread credit ratings system is limited in scope and not used in many daily financial transactions.

The social credit system also includes information on legal compliance, which acts as a proxy for an underdeveloped legal system. If legal compliance is not fully enforced by traditional institutions, a proxy for legal compliance, such as a social credit score that contains information about fraudulent activities, may help to fill this gap. Information about legal activities helps consumers and firms to make rational decisions in the marketplace. For example, if the tainted food and lead-paint toy scandals that rocked China in 2007-2008 could have been averted through a social credit system, this would have helped to maintain stability in market activity within these industries.

The question is, to what extent will individuals be rated based on opaque information that they cannot access, and to what extent will information used be relevant? The foreign media has stated that China will mine big data to rate citizens based on marketplace transactions and websites visited. So far this assertion cannot be confirmed by actual official policies. Information on individuals such as legal violations may, again, act as a proxy for a weak legal system. However, since it is up to individual institutions to carry out their own ratings, it appears that there will be a variation in the types of information gathered.

Some have argued that individuals will be rated based on purchases. Since many Chinese still use cash in marketplace transactions, the interpretation that grocery store and other daily transactions will be evaluated for credit scoring does not ring true. A small percentage of individuals currently shops on the internet, so internet purchases cannot be used for a national social credit program. It is possible for individuals to be rated based on Communist party membership or other political affiliations since that information is available, but it is not clear how and whether this will be used. For this policy, the devil is in the details, but it is obvious that when it comes to this new system the foreign media has jumped to conclusions that have little factual basis."

And of course I have to point out, that what is probably most significant about this article is the last section - and how quickly things have changed in the Chinese consumer marketplace: the volume of mobile payments for small and large purchases, as well as the volume of internet/online shopping, have both grown immensely in such an amazingly short period of time, to say the least!

Part Four:
The Chinese Social Credit System At Work

The Chinese Social Credit System –
Its System Architecture: An Overview

The Planning Outline For The Construction
Of A Social Credit System 2014-2020

In Depth Analyses Of The System's
Rollout Towards 2020

In looking at the Chinese Social Credit System at work, we look first at Wikipedia's detailed entry (as of July 5, 2018) about this subject, titled "Social Credit System".

It begins with this short introduction: "The Social Credit System (shehui xinyong t zi) is a proposed Chinese government initiative for developing a national reputation system. It has been reported to be intended to assign a 'social credit' rating to every citizen based on government data regarding their economic and social status. It works as a mass surveillance tool and uses big data analysis technology. In addition, it is also meant to rate businesses operating on the Chinese market."

Note: from what we've already seen, this isn't exactly an objective viewing of the stated intent of the Chinese Social Credit System – the stated intent being first and foremost a strong focus on restoring trust and honesty to the Chinese economic system – and along with that the Chinese social system. There is also a strong private effort involved in such a rating system. And initially at least, rating businesses is clearly not a secondary objective, since this is aimed primarily at bringing trust and faith to the economic system. So viewing it as a mass surveillance tool, initially at least, might be taking the development and use of early artificial intelligence and facial recognition technologies, as well as other tools for mass surveillance, just a little too far, at least in the relatively early phases we've examined and will be examining!

For a short overview of what we will be looking at in much greater detail, Wikipedia continues with this section of its entry:

"Planning Outline For The Construction Of A Social Credit System (2014-2020)

The Social Credit System is an example of China's 'top-level design' approach. It is coordinated by the Central Leading Group for Comprehensively Deepening Reforms." (This is footnoted to Mirjam Meissner's May 24, 2017 article that takes an in-depth look at China's Social Credit System for Merics.org, which we will be examining very closely later in this section.) And the entry continues, "According to the overall 'Planning Outline For The Construction Of A Social Credit System (2014-2020)' issued by the State Council, the Social Credit System will focus on four areas: 'honesty in government affairs', 'commercial integrity', 'societal integrity' and 'judicial credibility'. Media coverage has thus far focused mostly on the rating of individual citizens (which falls under 'societal integrity'). However, the Chinese government's plans go far beyond that and also include plans for credit scores for all businesses operating in China.

The Chinese government wants the basic structures of the Social Credit System to be in place by 2020. It is unclear whether the system will work as envisioned by then, but the Chinese government has fast-tracked the implementation of the Social Credit System, resulting in the publication of numerous policy documents and plans since the main plan was issued in 2014. If the Social Credit System is implemented as envisioned, it will constitute a new way of controlling both the behavior of individuals and businesses.

The main outline often mentioned in Western news outlet stories, the 'State Council Notice concerning Issuance of the Planning Outline for the Construction of a Social Credit System (2014-2020)', was issued by China's State Council on June 14, 2014. Rogier Creemers, a post-doctoral scholar at the Programme for Comparative Media Law and Policy at the University of Oxford, has posted a translation of the document." And we'll be taking an in-depth look at Mr. Creemers' highly significant translation next!

The Wikipedia entry continues, "The goal of the initiative according to the Planning Outline is 'raising the awareness for integrities and the level of credibility within society.' The Social Credit System is presented as an important means to perfect the 'socialist market economy' as well as strengthening and innovating governance of society. This indicated that the Chinese government views it both as an important means to regulate the economy and as a tool of governance to steer the behavior of citizens.

Among other things, the Social Credit System is meant to provide an answer to the problem of lack of trust on the Chinese market. Proponents argue that it will help eliminate problems such as food safety issues, cheating, and counterfeit goods. Building on that, China's officially defined aim is to enhance trust and social stability by creating a 'culture of sincerity'.

The Social Credit System will be limited to Mainland China and thus does not apply to Hong Kong and Macau. However, at present, plans do not distinguish between Chinese companies and foreign companies operating on the Chinese market, raising the possibility that foreign businesses will be subjected to the system as well.

The system has already been implicated in a number of controversies. Of particular note is how it is applied to individuals as well as companies. People have already faced various punishments for violating social protocols. The system has been used to already block nine million people with 'low scores' from purchasing domestic flights. While still in preliminary stages the system has been used to ban people and their children from certain schools, prevent low scorers from renting hotels, using credit cards, and blacklist individuals from being able to procure employment. The system has also been used to rate individuals for their internet habits (too much online gaming reduces one's score for example), personal shopping habits, and a variety of other personal and wholly innocuous acts that have no impact on the wider community. Criticism of this program has been widespread with the proposed system being described by Human Rights Watch as 'chilling' and filled with arbitrary abuses.

Progress Of Implementation

In 2015, the People's Bank of China licensed eight companies to begin trial credit systems. Among these eight firms are Sesame Credit, which belongs to the Alibaba Group, Tencent, as well as China's biggest ride sharing and dating firms, Didi Chuxing and Baihe.com respectively. In general, multiple firms are collaborating with the government to develop the system of software and algorithms.

While the government originally considered the Social Credit System's operation to be run by a private firm, it has since acknowledged the need for third party administration. In 2017, no licenses to private companies were granted. The reasons are conflicts of interest, the remaining control of the government, as well as the lacking cooperation in voluntary data sharing among the firms that participate in the development. However, the Social Credit System's operation by a seemingly external association, such as a formal collaborative between private firms, has not been ruled out yet. Private companies have also signed contracts with provincial governments to set up the basic infrastructure for the Social Credit System at the provincial level.

As of February 2018, no comprehensive nation-wide social credit system exists, but there are multiple pilots testing the system on a local level as well as in specific sectors of industry. One such program has been implemented in Shanghai through its Honest Shanghai app, which uses facial recognition software to browse government records, and rates users accordingly. Some reports have stated that the ratings may use information gathered from Chinese citizens' online behavior.

As of March 2017, 137 commercial credit reporting companies are active on the Chinese market. As part of the development of the Social Credit System, the Chinese government has been monitoring the progress of third-party Chinese credit rating systems.

In March 2018, Reuters reported that restrictions on citizens and businesses with low trustworthiness Social Credit ratings would come into effect on May 1st.

Sesame Credit

Currently most developed technology is provided by the Alibaba Group's Ant Financial which operates Sesame Credit. Alibaba is China's largest conglomerate of online services, including the largest online shopping and payment providers. Sesame Credit's scoring system is roughly modeled after FICO scoring in the United States and Schfa in Germany.

In 2015, Sesame Credit published information on the methodology behind its current running beta version.

Data Collection

The Chinese government aims at assessing the trustworthiness and compliance of each person. To achieve this, it collects data from all sources by utilizing the regulatory freedom it built: from objects and social networks, public and private institutions, and offline and online. Here, data stems both from people's own accounts, as well as their network's activities. Website operators can mine the traces of data that we leave and derive a full social profile, including e.g. people's location, friends, health records, insurance, private messages, financial situation, gaming duration, smart home statistics, preferred newspapers, shopping history, and dating behaviour.

The corporate network of Sesame Credit, led by the Alibaba Group, spans over insurance, loan, historical payment, dating, shopping and mobility data. Therefore, this system is powered by data from more than 300 million real-name registered users and 37 million small businesses that buy and sell on Alibaba Group marketplaces. Due to Sesame Credit's close collaboration with the government, it also has access to all public documents, such as official identity and financial records.

Further this also includes all information that the Chinese government is collecting under its data protection regulation, which requires businesses to turn over their data. For example, the government already has access to the messages of WeChat's 850 million active users, China's most popular communication application. Thus, China can already access and monitor most social and object data of its citizens on a continuous basis.

Data Structuring

A combination of big data, statistics and behavioral analytics sets the basis of China's Social Credit System. Automated algorithms are used to structure the collected data, based on government's rules that define good and bad. What remains unclear is whether data is also structured according to trustworthiness, to eliminate errors through fake news or unreliable sources. At Sesame Credit, data fragments are further classified into five categories:

1) Credit History: reflects users' past payment history and level of debt
2) Fulfillment Capacity: shows users' ability to fulfill contract obligations
3) Personal Characteristics: examine the extent and accuracy of personal information
4) Behavior and Preferences: reveal users online behavior
5) Interpersonal Relationships: reflect the online characteristics of a user's friends

To date, the specifications of the algorithm that determine the classification, as well as the analytical parameters and indicators, remain confidential.

Data Distribution

Sesame Credit emphasizes its strict privacy and data protection, ensured through encryption and segregation. The firm also states that data is only gathered upon knowledge and consent of the user. According to Ant Financial, users' scores can currently only be shared with their authorization or by themselves."

Note: nevertheless a person can't be faulted for being concerned about such aggregation of personal information, especially in an atmosphere – or a political system, where it would be very hard indeed for a private business to outright refuse any governmental request to provide such aggregated information! I don't think there can be any different expectation, no matter which credit services provider might be involved.

Data Visualization

The above-mentioned five categories that Sesame Credit classifies its data into, have different weightings attached to them. Based on those, an algorithm determines a citizen's final citizen score, ranked among others. The scores in the rankings range from 350 (lowest trustworthiness) to 950 (highest trustworthiness). From 600 up, one can gain privileges, while lower scores will revoke them. According to current plans, the final score and ranking will be publicly available.

And has been made very clear, there definitely are important implications of such high and low Social Credit rankings for the Chinese citizen – as well as for businesses.

Social Credit For Businesses

For business, the Social Credit System is meant to serve as a market regulation mechanism. The goal is to establish a self-enforcing regulatory regime fueled by big data in which businesses exercise 'self-restraint'. The basic idea is that with a functional credit system in place, companies will comply with government policies and regulations to avoid having their scores lowered.

As currently envisioned, companies with good credit scores will enjoy benefits such as good credit conditions, lower tax rates, and more investment opportunities. Companies with bad credit scores will potentially face unfavorable conditions for new loans, higher tax rates, investment restrictions, and lower chances to participate in publicly funded projects. Government plans also envision real-time monitoring of a business's activities. In that case, infractions on the part of a business could result in a lowered score almost instantly. However, whether this will happen depends on the future implementation of the system as well as on the availability of technology needed for this kind of monitoring."

And at this point, it's once again essential to interject a caveat into business scoring, since so much appears to ride on a good or bad rating: in such a system strong structures must be put into place that provide certain safeguards against false and malicious reports filed against businesses, in order to protect such businesses from "immoral and unethical" competitive business practices; and such structures must include sufficient resources and personnel availability, in order to promptly and effectively investigate appeals made against any such malicious and unfair efforts to damage competing businesses!

Now we come to what is likely the most important document going forward, in this examination of the Chinese Social Credit System experience: **Rogier Creemers' editing and translation of the "Planning Outline for the Construction of a Social Credit System (2014-2020)"** of June 14, 2014, and updated on April 25, 2015; and posted on China Copyright and Media at chinacopyrightand media.wordpress.com

This State Council document, and Mr. Creemers' translation, begins:

"A social credit system is an important component part of the Socialist market economy system and the social governance system. It is founded on laws, regulations, standards and charters. It is based on a complete network covering the credit records of members of society and credit infrastructure; it is supported by the lawful application of credit information and a credit services system, its inherent requirements are establishing the idea of a sincerity culture, and carrying forward sincerity and traditional virtues. It uses encouragement to keep trust, and constraints against breaking trust, as incentive mechanisms; and its objective is raising the honest mentality and credit levels of the entire society.

Accelerating the construction of a social credit system is an important basis for comprehensively implementing the scientific development view and building a harmonious Socialist society; it is an important method to perfect the Socialist market economy system, accelerating and innovating social governance; and it has an important significance for strengthening the sincerity consciousness of the members of society, forging a desirable credit environment, raising the overall competitiveness of the country and stimulating the development of society and the progress of civilization.

On the basis of the general requirement to 'strengthen sincerity in government affairs, commercial sincerity, social sincerity and judicial credibility construction' as put forward by the 18th Party Congress; 'establish and complete a social credit system, commend sincerity and punish insincerity' as put forward by the 3rd Plenum" (note: assembly of all members of a group or committee) "of the 18th Party Congress; 'establish and complete a social credit system' as put forward in the 'CCP Central Committee and State Council Opinions concerning Strengthening and Innovating Social Management'; as well as 'accelerate the construction of a social credit system' as put forward in the '12th Five-Year Planning Outline of the Economic and Social Development of the People's Republic of China' (hereafter simply named the '12th Five-Year Plan'), this Planning outline has been formulated. The planning period is 2014-2020.

I. The Overall Line Of Thinking For the Construction of A Social Credit System

1) Development Situation

The Party Centre and the State Council pay high regard to the construction of a social credit system. Relevant regions, departments and work units have explored and moved the matter forward, and positive headway has been made in social credit system construction. The State Council has established an interministerial joint conference for social credit system construction to comprehensively move social credit system construction forward, which promulgated and implemented the 'Credit Investigation Sector Management Regulations', and a batch of rules and standards for credit system construction have been successively rolled out.

A nationwide uniform financial credit information database has been created, the construction of a credit system for small and micro-enterprises and the countryside has been vigorously moved forward; various ministries have promoted credit information openness, launched industry credit evaluation, and implemented categorized supervision and management over credit; various sectors have vigorously launched propaganda and education on sincerity and sincerity self-discipline activities; various regions have explored the establishment of comprehensive credit information sharing platforms, stimulating the comprehensive use of credit information by various departments and work units; social demand for credit services and products is growing every day, and the credit services market is incessantly expanding in scale.

Although certain headway has been made in the construction of our country's social credit system, the contradictions that it is not matched, not coordinated and not adapted to economic development levels and the social development stage remain prominent. The main problems that exist include: a credit investigation system that covers all of society has not yet been formed; credit records of the members of society are gravely flawed; incentive mechanisms to encourage keeping trust and punishments for breaking trust are not complete; trust-keeping is insufficiently rewarded, the costs of breaking trust tend to be low; credit services markets are not developed, service systems are immature, there are no norms for service activities, the credibility of service bodies is insufficient, and the mechanisms to protect the rights and interests of credit information subjects are flawed; the social consciousness of sincerity and credit levels tend to be low, and a social atmosphere in which agreements are honoured and trust are honestly kept has not yet been shaped, especially grave production safety accidents, food and drug security incidents happen from time to time; commercial swindles, production and sales of counterfeit products, tax evasion, fraudulent financial claims, academic impropriety and other phenomenon cannot be stopped in spite of repeated bans, there is still a certain difference between the extent of sincerity in government affairs and judicial credibility, and the expectations of the popular masses.

2) Circumstances and Requirements

Our country is currently in the assault phase of deepening economic structural reform and perfecting the Socialist market economy system. The modern market economy is a credit economy; establishing and completing a social credit system is an important step in rectifying and standardizing the market economy order, improving the market's credit environment, reducing transaction costs and preventing economic risk; and is an urgent requirement to reduce administrative governmental interference in the economy and perfecting the Socialist market economy system.

Our country is in a period of strategic opportunity to accelerate the transformation (in) its development method and realize scientific development. Accelerating the promotion of social credit system construction is an important precondition for stimulating optimized resource allocation, broadening internal demand and stimulating the structural optimization and improvement of industrial structures, and is an urgent requirement to perfect scientific development mechanisms.

Our country is in a crucial period of economic and social transformation. Interest subjects are becoming more pluralized (special interest groups are multiplying), various social contradictions (conflicts) are prominent, and social organizations and management methods are seeing profound change. Completely moving the construction of a social credit system forward is an effective method to strengthen social sincerity, stimulate mutual trust in society, and reducing social contradictions (conflicts), and is an urgent requirement for strengthening and innovating social governance, and building a Socialist harmonious society.

Our country is in a period of expansion in which the openness levels of the economy are rising on an even greater scale, across even broader fields, and at even deeper levels. Economic globalization has enabled an incessant increase of our country's openness towards the world, and economic and social interaction with other countries and regions is becoming ever closer. Perfecting the social credit system is a necessary condition to deepen international cooperation and exchange, establishing international brands and reputations, reducing foreign-related transaction costs, and improving the country's soft power and international influence, and is an urgent requirement to promote the establishment of an objective, fair, reasonable and balanced international credit rating system, to adapt to the new circumstances of globalization and master new globalized structures.

3) Guiding Ideology and Target Principles

To comprehensively move the construction of a social credit system forward, we must persist in taking Deng Xiaoping Theory" (per Wikipedia, that means opening China to the world and advocating adapting past thinking to existing socio-economic conditions, and promoting political and economic pragmatism), "the important 'Three Represents' thought" (per Wikipedia, credited to Jiang Zemin in 2000, promoting the idea, as I understand it, that the Communist Party of China, in adapting to new situations and tasks, "should be representative to advanced social productive forces, advanced culture, and the interests of the overwhelming majority") "and the scientific development view as guidance, act according to the spirit of the 18th Party Congress, the 3rd Plenum of the 18th Party Congress, and the '12th Five-Year Plan', take completing credit laws, regulations and standard systems and shaping a credit investigation system covering all of society as the basis" (for developing the social credit system); "take moving forward the construction of sincerity in government affairs, commercial sincerity, social sincerity and judicial credibility as main content; take moving forward the construction of a sincerity culture and establishing mechanisms to encourage sincerity and punish insincerity as focal points; take moving forward the construction of sectoral credit, the construction of local credit and the development of credit service markets as support; take raising the entire society's sense of sincerity and credit levels and improving the economic and social operating environment as targets; put people first, broadly shape a thick atmosphere in the entire society that keeping trust is glorious and breaking trust is disgraceful, and ensure that sincerity and trustworthiness become conscious norms of action among all the people.

The main objectives of the construction of a social credit system are: by 2020, basically having established fundamental laws, regulations and standard systems for social credit; basically having completed a credit investigation system covering the entire society with credit information and resource sharing at the basis; basically having completed credit supervision and management systems, having a relatively perfect credit service market system, and giving complete rein to mechanisms to encourage keeping trust and punish breaking trust; having made clear headway in the construction of sincerity in government affairs, commercial sincerity, social sincerity and judicial credibility, and a substantial rise in market and social satisfaction levels; having broadly strengthened the sense of sincerity in the entire society; (the following will have been) achieved: a clear improvement in the credit environment for economic and social development, and a market improvement of the economic and social order.

The main principles for social credit system construction are:

Government promotion, joint construction with society.
Fully give rein to the organizational, guiding, promoting and demonstration roles of government. The government is responsible for formulating and implementing development plans, completing regulations and standards, fostering and supervising credit service markets. Focus on giving rein to the role of market mechanisms, coordinate and optimize resource allocation, encourage and muster social forces, broaden participation, move forward together, shape joint forces for social scredit system construction.

Completing the legal system, standardizing development.
Progressively establish and complete credit law and regulation systems and credit standards systems, strengthen credit information management, standardize the development of credit service structures, safeguard the security of credit information, and the rights and interests of information subjects.

Comprehensive planning, graduated implementation.
In view of the long-term nature, systemic nature and complexity of social credit system construction, strengthen top-level design, stand on the present, gaze toward the future, plan the overall picture comprehensively, plan systematically, organize implementation in a planned and graduated manner.

Breakthroughs in focus points, strengthen application.
Choose focus and model regions to launch credit construction demonstrations, vigorously spread the socialized application of credit products, stimulate the interaction, exchange, coordination and sharing of credit information, complete combined social credit reward and punishment mechanisms, construct a social credit environment of sincerity, self-discipline, trust-keeping and mutual trust.

II. Move Sincerity Construction Forward In Focus Areas

1) Accelerating the construction of government affairs sincerity

Sincerity in government affairs is the crux of social credit system construction. The level of sincerity of all sorts of governmental actors plays an important model and guidance role for the construction of sincerity among other social subjects.

Persisting in administration according to the law.
Administration according to the law penetrates the entire process of policymaking, implementation, supervision and service. Comprehensively move government affairs openness forward under the precondition of protecting information security, commercial secrets and individual privacy. Publish credit information obtained in administrative management according to the law, and establish effective information sharing mechanisms. Realistically raise government work efficiency and service levels, transform the functions of government. Complete systems to constrain and supervise the use of power, ensure that policymaking powers, implementation powers, and supervision powers are mutually constraining and mutually coordinating. Perfect mechanisms and procedures for government policymaking, raise the transparency of policymaking. Further expand the major policy decision publication and hearing system, broaden channels for public participation in government policymaking, strengthen social supervision over and constraints on the use of power, improve government credibility, establish an honest image of an open, fair and clean government.

Give rein to the demonstration role of government in sincerity construction. All levels (of) People's Governments must first and foremost strengthen their own sincerity construction, and drive the establishment of a sincerity consciousness in all of society and an increase in the levels of sincerity through honest governing by governments. Take the lead in using credit information and credit products in administrative permission, government procurement, tendering and bidding, labour and employment, social security, scientific research management, cadre promotion and appointment, management and supervision, application for government financial support and other such areas, and foster the development of a credit services market.

Accelerate the construction of government trust-keeping and commitment mechanisms. Strictly carry out the commitments that government has made to society, bring the honouring of agreements and keeping of service commitments in government affairs into the government achievements evaluation system, make development planning and government work reporting concerning the implementation situation of economic and social development objectives, as well as the situation of keeping commitments in handling affairs for the common people into an important content for evaluating the level of government honest, and promote the progressive establishment and completion of government affairs and administrative commitment-keeping assessment system in all localities and departments. All levels (of) People's Governments' political commitments and all categories of agreements signed according to the law must be earnestly carried out and honoured.

It is necessary to vigorously create a fair, competitive, uniform and highly efficient market environment. It is not permitted to engage in local protectionism measures, such as abusing administrative powers to close off markets, cover up or connive at acts violating laws, regulations or trust by social subjects within an administrative region. It is necessary to support statistics departments in creating statistics according to the law, and creating accurate statistics. Government borrowing must take place according to the law and regulations, appropriate in scope, with controllable risks and transparent procedures. Budget controls must be strengthened in government revenues and expenses, and transparency raised. Strengthen and perfect mass supervision and public opinion supervision mechanisms. Perfect government information sincerity restraint and accountability mechanisms. All levels (of) People's Governments must consciously accept legal supervision from that level's People's Congress and the democratic supervision and auditing strength of supervision, auditing and other such bodies concerning administrative acts.

Strengthen sincerity management and education among civil servants. Establish civil servant sincerity dossiers, enter civil servants' personal credit information concerning reports on events, records of sincerity and cleanliness in government affairs, the results of annual evaluations, acts violating laws, disciplines and contract into their files, and make civil servants' sincerity records into an important basis for assessment, employment and rewards. Deeply launch education concerning sincerity, abiding by the law and morality among civil servants, strengthen study of legal knowledge and credit knowledge, compile civil servants' sincerity manuals, strengthen the legal and sincerity consciousness of civil servants, establish a line of civil servant teams that abide by the law and by sincerity, are highly efficient and clean.

2) Deeply Move The Construction Of Commercial Sincerity Forward

Raising sincerity levels in commercial affairs is a focus point of the construction of the social credit system. It is a basic condition for commercial relations to be effectively upheld, commercial operating costs to effectively lower, and the commercial environment to effectively improve. It is the root for the existence of the substantial development of all kinds of commercial subjects, and is the basic guarantee for the effective conduct of all kinds of economic activities.

Credit construction in the area of production.
Build credit reporting structures for safe production, perfect safe production commitment. Build safe production credit record and safe production trust-breaking punishment systems. Take the mining, non-coal mining, hazardous chemical product, fireworks, and special equipment production enterprises as well as civil explosive product production and sales enterprises and demolition enterprises or work units as focus point, complete

safe production access and withdrawal credit examination and verification mechanisms, and stimulate enterprises to implement safe production responsibility systems. Take food, medicine, daily consumables, agricultural produce and farming inputs into focus points, to strengthen and perfect 12365 product quality input reporting and consulting service platforms, build systems for honest quality reporting, trust-breaking blacklist and exposure, market prohibition and withdrawal.

Credit construction in the logistics sector.
Research and formulate collection and sharing systems for enterprise credit information in the area of trading and logistics, perfect basic credit evaluation norms and indicator systems for trading and logistics enterprises. Move forward the construction of credit in wholesale and retail, trading and logistics, accommodations, food and drink and residents services, launch categorized enterprise credit management.

Perfect credit cooperation models between retailers and suppliers. Strengthen anti-monopoly and anti-fair competition law enforcement, strengthen investigation and prosecution of acts of market distortion, false propaganda, commercial swindling, commercial slander, commercial bribes and other such unlawful acts; expose model cases and major cases (to) increase the costs for enterprises to break trust, and stimulate sincere business and fair competition.

Progressively establish nationwide product circulation tracing systems with product bar codes and other such symbols as a basis. Strengthen the construction of sincerity systems for quality and health inspection. Support commerce and trade services enterprises' credit funding; develop commercial factoring, standardize advance payment and consumption acts. Encourage enterprises to broaden credit selling, stimulate individuals to consume on credit.

Move forward with the construction of credit in external commerce and trade. Further strengthen credit information management, credit risk monitoring and advance warning, as well as enterprise credit ranking management in foreign trade, foreign aid, foreign investment cooperation and other such areas. With the aid of electronic port management platforms, establish and perfect import and export enterprise credit evaluation systems, credit category management and joint supervision and management systems.

Credit construction in the area of finance.
Innovate financial credit products, improve financial services, safeguard the security of personal information of financial consumers, and protect the lawful rights and interests of financial consumers. Strengthen punishment of financial swindles, malicious evasion of loan repayments, insider trading, selling fake warranties, insurance and compensation fraud, disclosure of false information, illegal fundraising, obtaining foreign currency

under false pretenses and other acts of financial trust-breaking, and standardize the order of financial markets. Strengthen the construction of financial credit information infrastructure, further broaden the coverage of credit records, and strengthen the incentivizing role of the financial sector to those keeping trust, and its constraining role towards trust-breakers.

Credit construction in the area of taxation.
Establish intradepartmental credit information sharing mechanisms. Launch the exchange, verification and application of basic information about taxpayers, all kinds of trading information, asset ownership and transfer information as well as taxation records and other such tax-related kinds of information. Further perfect tax payment information ranking evaluation and publication systems, strengthen credit categorization management in the area of taxation, and give rein to the role of credit evaluation differentials in rewarding or punishing taxpayers. Establish black-list systems for legal violations concerning taxation. Move forward the joint management of taxation information and other kinds of social information and ensure that taxpayers comply with fiscal law.

Credit construction in the area of pricing.
Guide enterprises and businesses to strengthen self-discipline in pricing, standardize and guide businesses' pricing acts. Implement systems for businesses to clearly indicate their prices and fees, and strive for 'clear real prices'. Supervise and urge businesses in strengthening internal pricing management, establish and complete internal pricing management systems on the basis of the condition of business. Perfect business pricing sincerity systems, complete information disclosure work, and promote realistic reward and punishment systems. Strengthen pricing law enforcement inspection and anti-monopoly law enforcement; investigate and prosecute the concoction and dissemination of price rising information, pricing swindles, pricing monopolies and other such trust-breaking activities in pricing; openly expose model cases, and standardize the market pricing order.

Credit construction in the area of project construction.
Move credit system construction forward in the project construction market. Accelerate the construction for credit regulation systems in the project construction market, and formulate credit standards for all kinds of subjects and employees in the project construction market. Move forward the construction of a credit openness and sincerity system for project construction information, completely establish programme information and credit information openness and sharing columns on governmental websites; concentrate open project construction programme information and credit information, promote the construction of nationwide comprehensive search platforms, and realize 'one-stop' comprehensive search services for project construction programme information and credit information openness and sharing.

Deeply launch the construction of project quality and sincerity. Perfect entry and withdrawal structures for the project construction market, and strengthen punishment against enterprises where major project quality or security accidents occur, or other major trust-breaking acts occur, as well as (for) their employees. Establish connected management mechanisms linking credit evaluation result, qualification examination and approval, professional qualification registration, qualification cancellation, and other such examination, approval and verification procedures for enterprises and employees. Establish scientific and effective employee credit evaluation mechanisms and trust-breaking liability prosecution systems for the construction area, and bring dismembered contracting, out-contracting, unlawful sub-contracting, late payment of project funds and peasant worker salaries, etc., into the scope of liability for trust-breaking.

Credit construction in the area of government procurement.
Strengthen government procurement credit management, strengthen joint mechanisms, and protect the lawful rights and interests of parties in government procurement. Formulate credit record standards for suppliers, evaluation experts, government procurement agencies as well as corresponding employees. Establish records for bad conduct by government procurement suppliers according to the law, and prohibit suppliers with a record of bad conduct to participate in government procurement activities for a certain period of time. Perfect access and withdrawal mechanisms for the government procurement market, fully use the credit information provided by commerce and industry, taxation, finance, prosecutorial and other such departments to strengthen credit management of government procurement parties and corresponding personnel. Accelerate the construction of nationwide, uniform government procurement management and trading systems, raise the transparency of government procurement activities, and realize the uniform publication and sharing of credit information.

Credit construction in the area of tendering and bidding.
Broaden the scope of information openness and sharing concerning tendering and bidding, establish credit evaluation indicators and evaluation standard systems covering tendering and bidding situations, and complete credit information openness and sharing systems for tendering and bidding. Further implement recording and publication rules for unlawful acts in the tendering and bidding process, and promote the perfection of joint reward and punishment mechanisms. Realize the interaction and interconnection of tendering and bidding contract implementation and other such credit information, as well as real-time exchange, integration and sharing, with the use of electronic tendering and bidding systems and public service platforms; encourage market subjects to utilize basic credit information and third party credit evaluation results, and make them into an important basis for inspecting the credentials of and evaluating bidders, deciding on contracts and signing contracts.

Credit construction in the area of traffic and transportation.
Shape a traffic and transportation credit regulation system by integrating departmental regulations and local regulations and government rules. Perfect credit assessment standards, implement categorized assessment, supervision and management. Formulate assessment standards aimed at the different operational categories of public roads, railways, waterways, aviation, channels and other such transportation markets; strengthen credit assessment, evaluation, supervision and management, vigorously guide third-party bodies to participate in credit assessment and evaluation, progressively establish a comprehensive assessment and evaluation system that integrates traffic and transportation management bodies with social credit evaluation bodies, and that contains supervision, complaints and redress mechanisms.

List all kinds of unlawful traffic, and transportation acts into trust-breaking records. Encourage and support all work units to give preference to choose traffic and transportation enterprises and employees with high credit assessment ratings in areas such as purchasing traffic and transportation services, tendering and bidding, personnel management, etc. It is necessary to strengthen supervision, management and punishment of trust-breaking enterprises and employees, and progressively establish cross-regional and cross-sectoral credit reward and punishment mechanisms.

Credit construction in the area of e-commerce.
Build and complete e-commerce enterprise and client credit management and transaction credit evaluation systems, strengthen quality supervision by e-commerce enterprises of credit products they exploit and sell. Carry out the e-commerce subject identification rules, perfect website real-name systems. Strengthen website product quality inspection, strictly investigate and prosecute the production and sale of counterfeit goods, pyramid selling, false advertising, selling seconds as top-quality, violation of service contracts and other such swindling activities in the area of e-commerce. Attack inside-outside collusion, counterfeiting of flow rates and commercial reputation acts, and establish fixed-term sectoral prohibition rules for subjects breaking trust. Stimulate the broad application of e-commerce credit products in e-commerce. Launch trustworthiness authentication service work among e-commerce websites, spread the application of website trustworthiness symbols, and provide methods for e-commerce users to distinguish the real from the fake, and to recognize phishing websites.

Credit construction in the area of statistics.
Launch sincere statistics commitment activities among enterprises, create a fine wind of sincere reporting being glorious and trust-breaking and reporting falsehoods being disgraceful. Perfect statistical sincerity evaluation standard systems. Establish and complete sincerity evaluation structures for enterprise statistics and sincerity files for statistical personnel. Strengthen law enforcement and inspection, strengthen investigation

and prosecution of fraudulent acts in the area of statistics, and establish structures to report and expose trust-breaking acts in statistics. Expand joint punishment of enterprises breaking trust concerning statistics. Enter the name list files of enterprises breaking trust in statistics and information about their breach of laws and regulations into the credit information systems of finance, industry and commerce and other such sectors and departments; directly couple statistics credit records with enterprise finances, government subsidies, industry and commerce registration and other such measures, and realistically strengthen punishment and constraint of trust-breaking acts in statistics.

Credit construction in the intermediary services sector.
Establish and perfect credit records and exposure systems for intermediary services bodies and their employees, and make them into an important basis for administrative market law enforcement departments' carrying out categorized credit management. Focus on strengthening the management of notarization and arbitration, lawyers, accountancy, guarantees, authentication, inspection and monitoring, evaluation, accreditation, agency, brokerage, professional recommendation, consulting, trading and other such bodies, and explore the establishment of scientific and rational evaluation indicator systems, evaluation structures and work mechanisms.

Credit construction in the areas of exhibitions and advertising.
Promote sincere exhibition-running among exhibition organizing bodies, carry out the sincere service contract, establish structures to expose credit files and information about enterprises breaking laws and regulations, and broaden the application of credit services and products. Strengthen the construction of sincerity in the advertising sector, establish and complete categorized credit management structures for the advertising sector, attack all kinds of false advertising, give prominence to the responsibility of participants in advertising production and dissemination, and perfect trust-breaking punishment mechanisms for advertising subjects and eliminate mechanisms for grave trust-breaking.

Constructing sincerity management systems in enterprises.
Launch sincerity commitment activities in enterprises in all sectors; strengthen propaganda about enterprises that are models of sincerity, and exposure of model cases of trust-breaking; guide enterprises to strengthen their sense of social responsibility, strengthen credit self-discipline in production and operations, financial management and labour management, and improve the commercial ecology environment.

Encourage enterprises to establish client files and launch client sincerity evaluation; enter sincere trading records of clients into receivable account management and credit issuance quota calculations for credit sales, establish scientific enterprises credit management workflows, prevent credit risks, and enhance enterprises' comprehensive competitiveness. Strengthen enterprises' sincerity and contract compliance in debt issuance, lending, guarantees and other activities concerning debts, liabilities, credit trading, production and operations. Encourage and support enterprises meeting conditions to establish credit supervisors. Encourage enterprises to establish internal staff sincerity assessment and evaluation structures. Strengthen the credit self-construction of enterprises in water supply, electricity supply, heating supply, gas supply, telecommunications, railways, aviation and other sectors that relate to the popular masses' daily lives.

(3) Comprehensively move forward the construction of social sincerity.

Social sincerity is the basis for building the social credit system, only if there is mutual sincere treatment between members of society; and only if sincerity is fundamental, will it be possible to create harmonious and amicable interpersonal relationships; will it be possible to stimulate the progress of society and civilization, and realize social harmony, stability and a long period of peace and order.

Credit construction in the areas of healthcare, hygiene and birth control.
Strengthen the construction of credit management and sincere sectoral work styles in healthcare and hygiene bodies. Establish a value view of sincerity, and sincerity among skillful physicians, and persist in the professional integrity of benevolence in heart and deeds. Foster ideas about sincerity in work, sincerity in purchasing, sincerity in diagnosis and treatment, sincerity in fee charging and sincerity in healthcare protection; persist in reasonable examinations, reasonable use of medicine, reasonable treatment, reasonable fee charging and other such service norms in sincere healthcare.

Comprehensively establish publication systems for drug prices and healthcare service prices, launch foundational activities for sincere hospitals and sincere pharmacies, formulate credit evaluation indicators and standards for healthcare bodies and professional doctors, pharmacists, nurses and other healthcare personnel, and move forward with examination and evaluation of hospitals and the regular assessment of doctors, launch comprehensive evaluation of the medical deontology (sense of moral obligation, ethics, commitment) of healthcare personnel; punish unlawful and trust-breaking acts such as taking bribes, excessive treatments, etc., and establish a sincere healthcare service system.

Accelerate the perfection of credit structures in the area of drug security, establish credit files for drug research, development, production and circulation enterprises. Vigorously launch sincerity commitment activities for drug safety with 'sincerity is supreme, score successes with quality' as focus point, realistically raise credit supervision and management levels concerning drug security, strictly attack acts of counterfeiting and falsification, and guarantee that the popular masses use drugs in a safe and effective manner. Strengthen credit construction in the area of population and birth control, and launch credit information sharing work in population and birth control.

Credit construction in the area of social security.
Establish comprehensive sincerity systems in areas such as disaster relief, aid, care for the elderly, social security, charity, lotteries, etc. Attack all kinds of trust-breaking acts such as swindling and deception. Establish and complete sincerity systems in all segments, such as application, verification and withdrawal concerning the implementation of policies affecting people's livelihoods, such as social aid, social housing, etc.

Strengthen the verification of conditions for applications in policies concerning people's livelihoods. Strengthen dynamic management for social aid and supervision and management for the use of social housing, and put individuals breaking trust and violating regulations on a credit blacklist.

Build information systems for the verification of residents' and households' economic situation; establish and perfect authentication mechanisms for low income households, guarantee that social aid, social housing and other such policies concerning the people's livelihood are carried out in a fair, just and healthy manner. Establish and complete social security management systems. Strengthen management in social security, strengthen labour guarantees and supervision of law enforcement in the area of social security; standardize benefits payments activities, strengthen punishment for acts violating regulations, cheating or deceiving insurance, etc. by all kinds of social security hospitals, pharmacies, industrial injury insurance-funded healthcare bodies and other social security bodies as well as their work personnel; prevent and attack all kinds of insurance fraud.

Further perfect social security finance management systems. Raise the transparency of fee collection, management, payment and all other segments. Promote the construction of sincerity systems in social insurance, standardize the payment acts of those participating in the insurance, and guarantee the safe operation of social security funds.

Credit construction in the area of labour and employment.
Further implement and perfect the structure for sincerity and legal compliance concerning labour guarantees in enterprises, formulate rules to publicize major unlawful acts concerning labour guarantees to society. Establish systems to publicize unlawful acts by employing work units concerning wages payment arrears, and complete hierarchical credit evaluation rules for labour guarantees in employing work units. Standardize employment activities, strengthen management of the implementation and mediation of

labour contracts, promote that enterprise vigorously launch activities to build harmonious labour guarantees.

Strengthen supervision and law enforcement of labour guarantees, and strengthen the attack against unlawful acts. Strengthen the construction of sincerity in the human resources market, standardize the activities of professional intermediaries, attack all kinds of unlawful and trust-breaking activities of black(listed) intermediaries, black(listed) employers, etc.

Credit construction in the area of education and scientific research.
Strengthen education about sincerity among educational and research personnel. Launch activities concerning sincerity commitments among teachers, and consciously accept supervision by the broad students, parents and all walks of society. Give rein to the influential role of teachers in education about sincerity and being a model of virtue for others. Strengthen education about sincerity among students, foster good habits of sincerity and trust-keeping, and lay the basis to raise the sincerity and quality of the entire nation.

Explore the establishment of credit evaluation systems for education bodies and their employees, teachers and students, research bodies and scientific and technological communities, as well as research personnel; link up credit evaluation with examinations and student recruitment, student status management, grant of degrees and transcripts, research programme establishment, the professional evaluation of specialized technological position, appointment and employment award selection, etc. Strive to resolve the problems that schooling records are fabricated, dissertations are plagiarized, there is academic impropriety, there is fraud in examinations and student recruitment, etc.

Credit construction in the areas of culture, sports and tourism.
With the support of the nationwide cultural market technological supervision, management and public service platforms, establish and complete credit information databases of cultural enterprise subjects, employees and cultural products in areas such as entertainment, performance, artworks, online culture, etc. Formulate management measures for sincerity in cultural markets according to the law, and strengthen dynamic supervision and management in cultural markets.

Formulate credit employment standards for professional sports employees, establish rules for third-party evaluation of credit rankings of professional sports employees, professional sports clubs and intermediary organizations; move forward the broad utilization of corresponding credit information records and credit ranking in participating in or organizing professional sports matches, professional sports access and transfer sessions, etc.

Formulate sincerity service norms for professional tourism personnel, establish open customer feedback and complaints recording structures for the tourism industry; establish third-party evaluation systems for credit ranking of travel companies, tourism destinations, hotels, restaurants, etc.

Credit construction in the area of intellectual property rights.
Establish and complete intellectual property rights sincerity management structures, and publish credit evaluation rules for intellectual property protection. Focus on attacking infringement of intellectual property rights and the sale of fake and shoddy products, bring intellectual property rights infringement acts into trust-breaking records, strengthen the joint punishment of piracy, infringement, and raise the intellectual property rights protection consciousness of the website society. Launch credit construction among intellectual property service bodies, explore the establishment of various kinds of standard-setting systems and sincerity evaluation systems for intellectual property rights services.

Credit construction in the areas of environmental protection and energy saving.
Move forward the construction of state capabilities for environmental monitoring, information and statistics; strengthen the collection and integration of environmental protection work, perfect open catalogues of environment information. Establish open structures for environmental management and survey information. Perfect liability investigation mechanisms for environmental assessment documents, establish sincerity file databases for environmental assessment bodies, their employees and evaluation experts; strengthen categorized supervision and management over credit assessment of environmental bodies, their employees and evaluation experts.

Establish structures for enterprises to launch self-monitoring of the pollutions they emit, publish the situation of their pollution emissions, as well as to discover and deal with sudden incidents. Establish credit evaluation structures for enterprises' environmental behaviour, regularly publish evaluation results, and organize the carrying out of dynamic and categorized management; issue corresponding rewards, warnings and punishments on the basis of the enterprises' credit rank. Perfect credit information sharing mechanisms for enterprises' environmental activities, and strengthen links with banks, securities, insurance, commercial and other such departments.

Strengthen the construction of capacity to report and analyse statistics and data on national energy use. Strengthen the assessment of focus work units' responsibilities concerning their energy use targets, regularly publish assessment results, and research the establishment of credit evaluation mechanisms for focus work units. Strengthen energy auditing, energy saving evaluation and reporting mechanisms, as well as evaluation and supervision of employees' credit. Research the carrying out of energy saving service companies' credit evaluation work, and progressively publish credit evaluation results to society in a regular manner. Strengthen credit assessment and management concerning environmental project evaluation experts' employment situations.

Sincerity construction in social organizations.
With the support of legal person work unit information resource databases, accelerate the perfection of social organization registration and management information. Complete social organization information openness systems, guide social organizations to enhance the openness and transparency of their operations, and standardize the information openness behaviour of social organizations. Include sincerity construction content into the articles of association of all kinds of social organizations, strengthen the sincerity self-discipline of social organizations and raise the credibility of social organizations. Give rein to the role of social organizations (and commercial organizations) in the construction of sectoral credit, and strengthen members' sincerity propaganda, education and training.

Credit construction among natural persons.
Give prominence to the fundamental role of natural persons' credit construction in the construction of a social credit system. With the support of national population information resource databases, establish and perfect credit records for natural persons in economic and social life; and realize that natural persons' credit records are completely covered on a nationwide scale. Strengthen professional credit construction among focus groups; establish personal credit records among public servants, enterprises' legal representatives, lawyers, accounting employees, registered accountants, statistics employees, registered tax advisors, auditors, evaluators, and authentication, monitoring and survey employees, securities and futures employees, high-level managers in publicly traded companies, insurance brokers, medical personnel, teachers, scientific research personnel, patent service employees, project managers, news and media employees, tourist guides, professional veterinarians and other such persons, and record their credit ranking, broaden the use of professional credit reports, and guide to construction of professional ethics and behavioural norms.

Credit construction in the area of Internet applications and services.
Forcefully move forward the construction of online sincerity; foster ideas of running the Internet according to the law and using the Internet in a sincere manner, progressively implement the online real-name system, perfect legal guarantees for the construction of online credit, forcefully move forward the construction of online credit supervision and management mechanisms. Establish online credit evaluation systems, evaluate the credit of the operational behaviour of Internet enterprises and the online behaviour of netizens, and record their credit rank.

Establish network credit files covering Internet enterprises and individual netizens, vigorously move forward with the establishment of exchange and sharing mechanisms for online credit information and corresponding credit information in other areas; forcefully promote the broad application of online credit information in various areas of society. Establish online credit blacklist systems, list enterprises and individuals engaging in online swindles, rumourmongering, infringement of other persons' lawful rights and interests, and other grave acts of breaking trust online onto blacklists, adopt measures against subjects listed on blacklists including limitation of online conduct and barring sectoral access, and report them to corresponding departments for publication and exposure.

4) Forcefully move forward the construction of judicial credibility

Judicial credibility is an important content of the construction of a social credit system. It is a precondition to establish the judiciary's authority, and is a baseline for social public justice.

Construction of judicial credibility.
Increase the informatization levels of judicial trials, and realize interaction and interconnection of trial information between the four levels of the judiciary, covering the entire process of trial work. Move forward with information openness on the enforcement of cases, perfect joint enforcement mechanisms, and raise the enforcement of valid legal writs. Give rein to the functional role of trials to encourage sincere trading and advocate mutual trust and cooperation, punish commercial swindles, willful violation or breach of contracts and other such trust-breaking acts, and lead a wind of sincerity and trust-keeping.

Construction of prosecutorial credibility.
Further deepen prosecutorial openness, innovate methods and channels for prosecutorial openness, broadly hear the opinions of the masses, safeguard the popular masses' right to know, right to participate, right of expression and right to supervision with regard to prosecutorial work.

Continue to push forward 'sunshine care-handling', straighten management systems, strengthen internal and external supervision, establish and complete special investigation, synchronized supervision and responsibility prosecution mechanisms. Fully give rein to the functional role of legal supervision to strengthen the investigation and prevention of workplace crime, and stimulate the construction of sincerity; perfect systems to inquire about bribery cases, standardize and strengthen inquiry work management, establish and complete joint social mechanisms to inquire into and use bribery files.

Construction of credibility in the area of public security.
Comprehensively carry out 'sunshine law enforcement', publish law enforcement case-handling rules, structures, procedures, time limits and other such information according to the law; and in a timely manner, where there is information that should not be published to society because case-handling is still in progress, but relates to specific rights and obligations, or it is necessary that specific counterparts are aware of it, those specific counterparts shall be notified, or inquiry services shall be provided to those specific counterparts.

Further strengthen exchange and sharing of population information with all localities, and all departments. Perfect the construction of national population information resource databases. Enter citizens' traffic safety and law-breaking situation into sincerity files, stimulate all members of society to raise their consciousness about traffic security. Regularly publish the evaluation results of fire safety in high-fire risk work units to society, and make them into an important reference basis to rank work units' credit. Bring social work units' respect for fire safety laws and regulations into sincerity management, and strengthen the subjective responsibility of social work units concerning fire safety.

The construction of credibility in the judicial and administrative systems.
Further raise the standardization and institutionalization levels of management of prisons, drug rehabilitation facilities, and community correction bodies; safeguard the lawful rights and interests of persons serving sentences, persons rehabilitating from drug use, and persons in community correction. Forcefully move forward judicial and administrative information openness, further standardize and innovate information management and disclosure methods concerning lawyers, notaries, grassroots legal services, legal aid, judicial examinations, judicial expert advice, etc., and guarantee the popular masses' right to know.

Credit construction among judicial law enforcement and employed personnel.
Deepen the reform of the judicial system and work mechanisms, move forward the construction of law enforcement standardization, straighten law enforcement procedures, persist in the fact that laws must be obeyed, law-breaking must be punished and everyone is equal according to the law; raise the scientific, institutionalization and standardization levels of judicial work.

Fully give rein to the supervisory role of People's Congresses, Consultative Conferences and the social public over judicial work. Perfect mutual supervision and restraint mechanisms between judicial bodies, strengthen internal supervision in judicial bodies, and realize that supervision stimulates fairness, justice and credibility.

III) Strengthen the construction of sincerity education and a sincerity culture

The construction of sincerity education and a sincerity culture are major channels to lead the sincerity and self-discipline members of society, and enhance the moral cultivation of the members of society; and is an important content of the construction of the Socialist core value system.

1) Popularize sincerity education.

With constructing the Socialist core value system, fostering and practicing the Socialist core value view as the foundation; bring sincerity education into the entire process of civil virtue construction and spiritual civilization construction. Move forward the civil virtue construction project, strengthen education about social morals, professional ties, household values and individual morality, inherit the fine traditional virtues of China, carry forward the new winds of the times, and shape a fine trend of 'seeing sincerity and trust-keeping as glorious, and seeing the loss of integrity to temptation and gains as shameful' across the entire society.

Further enhance the content of sincerity education in all levels and all kinds of education and training. Forcefully launch activities to let universal education and propaganda about credit enter enterprises, enter classrooms, enter communities, enter villages and enter households.

Build and use morality classrooms well, and advocate value views and moral norms of patriotism, respecting labour, sincerity, amity, etc. Launch mass activities for moral judgment, conduct analysis and evaluation of instances where there was a lack of sincerity and credit was not stressed, and guide people towards sincerity and trust-keeping, morality and upholding courtesy.

2) Strengthen the construction of a sincerity culture.

Carry forward a culture of sincerity with members of society as targets, with sincerity propaganda as method and with sincerity education as carrier, forcefully advocate sincerity and ethical norms, carry forward the positive and upward, sincere and trust-keeping traditional culture of the Chinese nation and the contract spirit of the modern market economy, and shape social morals of venerating sincerity and practicing sincerity.

Establish models of sincerity. Fully give rein to the propaganda and guiding roles of television, radio, newspapers, the Internet and other such media; integrate the selection of models of virtues and all kinds of sectoral sincerity construction of activities, establish social credit models, ensure that members of society have examples to learn from, goals to pursue and that sincerity and trust-keeping become conscious pursuits of the entire society.

Deeply launch topical activities concerning sincerity. Organize public interest activities such as the 'Sincerity Activity Week', 'Quality Month', 'Safe Production Month', 'Sincere Trading Propaganda Week', the '5 March' Lei Feng Activity Day, the '15 March' International Consumer Rights Protection Day, the '14 June' Credit Record Care Day, the '4 December' National Legal System Propaganda Day, etc. In a paced and planned manner, give prominence to the topic of sincerity; create a social atmosphere of sincerity and harmony.

Forcefully launch special campaigns in focus sectors and areas on the question of sincerity. Deeply launch specialized education and campaign activities concerning prominent issues in the area of morality; launch special campaigns targeting sectors and areas where sincerity is prominently lacking and sincerity building is urgently necessary; persist in correcting unhealthy trends and evil practices of abusing power for personal gain, lying and cheating, forgetting integrity when tempted by gains, benefitting oneself at others' expense, etc., and establish trends of sectoral sincerity and integrity.

3) Accelerate the training of specialized credit talents.

Strengthen the construction of the scholarly specialization of credit management. List credit management as an emerging and focus discipline that is urgently needed for the reform of the national economic system and the development of social governance; support higher education institutes meeting conditions to establish credit management majors and to set up corresponding courses, and establish credit management research streams in graduate student programmes. Launch research in credit theory, credit management, credit technology, credit standards, credit policy and other such areas.

Strengthen professional credit management training and specialized evaluation. Establish and complete professional credit management training and specialized evaluation structures. Expand professional qualification training for credit management, train specialized forces for credit management. Stimulate and strengthen the circulation and training of credit employees and credit management personnel, to provide human resource support for the construction of a social credit system.

IV) Accelerate the construction and application of credit information systems

Completing credit records of members of society is a basic requirement for the construction of a social credit system. Giving rein to the strengths and roles of sectors, localities and markets, accelerating the construction of the social credit system, and perfecting the recording, integration and application of credit information, are the basis and the preconditions for shaping mechanisms to encourage trust-keeping and punish trust-breaking.

1) The construction of sectoral credit information systems.

Strengthen credit record construction in focus areas. Focus on the areas of industry and commerce, tax payment, pricing, import and export, production safety, product quality, environmental protection, food and drugs, medicine and healthcare, intellectual property rights, logistical services, project construction, e-commerce, traffic and transportation, contract fulfillment, human resources, social security, education and research, and perfect sectoral credit record and employee credit files.

Establish sectoral credit information databases. All departments must make data standardization and application standardization into principles, rely on the State's various major informatization projects, integrate intra-sectoral credit information resources, ensure the electronic storage of credit records, accelerate the construction of credit information services, and accelerate the interconnection and interactivity of credit information between sectors. All sectors must respectively take responsibility for the organization and publication of credit information within those sectors.

2) The construction of local information systems.

Accelerate the integration of government affairs credit information. All localities must record, perfect and integrate the credit information generated in the process of carrying out public management duties by all departments and work units in the locality. Shape uniform credit information sharing platforms, and provide convenient ways for enterprises, individuals and social credit investigation bodies to consult government affairs credit information.

Strengthen the application of credit information within localities. All localities must formulate government affairs credit information openness catalogues, and shape information openness supervision systems. Forcefully move forward with government affairs credit information exchange and sharing of all departments and all localities within the locality, strengthen the application of credit information in public management, and raise operational efficiency.

3) The construction of credit investigation systems.

Accelerate the construction of credit investigation systems. Credit investigation bodies launching credit investigation shall build credit investigation systems targeting enterprise and undertaking work units as well as other social organizations and individuals; collect, arrange, store and process credit information of enterprise and undertaking work units and other social organizations, as well as individuals, according to the law, and adopt reasonable measures to ensure the accuracy of credit information. All localities and all sectors must support the establishment of credit investigation systems by credit investigation bodies.

Externally provide specialized credit investigation services. Credit investigation bodies must, on the basis of market demands, externally provide specialized credit investigation services, to move credit service product innovation forward in an orderly manner. Establish, complete and strictly implement rules and structures for internal risk prevention, avoidance of conflicts of interests and to ensure information security, provide convenient, rapid and efficient credit information services to users, and further broaden the application of credit reports in many areas, including the banking sector, the securities sector, the insurance sector, administrative law enforcement by government departments, etc.

4) The construction of uniform credit investigation platforms in the financial sector.

Perfect basic databases for financial credit information. Continue to move forward with the construction of basic databases for financial credit information, enhance data quality, perfect systemic functions, strengthen management over the secure operations of systems, further expand the coverage scope of credit reports, and enhance external service levels of systems.

Promote the construction of uniform credit investigation platforms in the financial sector. Continue to promote the linkage of credit information systems between financial management departments for banks, securities, insurance, foreign exchange, etc. Promote the construction of uniform credit information platforms in the financial sector, and move forward credit information exchange and sharing between financial supervision and management departments.

5) Move forward credit information exchange and sharing.

Progressively move forward government affairs credit information exchange and sharing. All localities and all sectors must establish credit information exchange and sharing mechanisms, comprehensively plan the use of existing credit information systems and infrastructure, move forward the interconnection and interactivity of various credit information systems and the exchange and sharing of credit information, and progressively create credit information networks that cover all information subjects, all credit information categories, and all regions nationwide, in a manner that is guided by needs, and under the preconditions of protecting privacy, clarifying responsibilities and ensuring the timeliness and accuracy of data. All sectors' controlling departments must conduct categorized and hierarchical management of credit information and determine their powers of inquiry; in inquiry concerning special cases, a special application must be made.

Move forward information exchange and sharing between the government affairs credit information system and credit investigation systems. Give rein to the role of market incentive mechanisms to encourage social finance bodies to strengthen integration with open government affairs credit information and non-government affairs credit information, to establish credit investigation service and product needs of a multi-layered, diverse and specialized society.

V) Perfect operational mechanisms for the social credit system with rewards as the focus point.

Operational mechanisms are the institutional basis to guarantee the coordinated operation of all parts of the social credit system. In particular, mechanisms encouraging trust-keeping and punishing breach of trust directly play a role in the credit activities of all social subjects, and are the core mechanisms for the operation of the social credit system.

1) Build mechanisms to incentivize trust-keeping and punish trust-breaking.

Strengthen rewards and incentives for subjects to keep trust. Expand rewards and propaganda strength for trust-keeping acts. Grant rewards to enterprises and model individuals keeping trust according to regulations, broadly propagate them through news media, and forge a public opinion environment that trust-keeping is glorious. Development and reform, finance, banking, environmental protection, housing and urban construction, traffic and transportation, commercial, industrial, fiscal, quality inspection, security supervision, customs, intellectual property rights and other such departments must, in the process of market supervision and public service, deepen the application of credit information and credit products, and extend 'green path' support and incentive mechanisms, such as preferential management, simplifying procedures, etc., to those keeping trust.

Strengthen restraint and punishment of subjects breaking trust. Strengthen administrative supervision, restraint and punishment. On the basis of the current administrative punishment measures, complete punishment structures for breach of trust, establish blacklist systems and market withdrawal mechanisms in all sectors. Promote all levels' People's Governments to implement categorized credit management, implement categorized credit supervision and management concerning market supervision and management, public service market access, qualification accreditation, administrative examination and approval, policy support and other areas, integrate the categories and levels of supervision and management counterparts to ensure that those breaking trust as punished.

Progressively establish systems for credit commitment by administrative approval applicants, and launch inspections of applicants' credit, ensure that applicants have credit records in government-recommended credit investigation bodies, coordinate with credit investigation bodies in launching credit information collection work.

Promote the creation of marketized constraint and punishment. Formulate normative credit evaluation standard systems and evaluation methods, perfect systems to record and expose information concerning trust-breaking, ensure that those breaking trust are constrained in their market interactions.

Promote the creation of sectoral constraints and punishments. Formulate sectoral self-discipline norms through sectoral associations and supervise members in obeying them. Implement warning, intra-sectoral reporting and criticism, open condemnation and other such punitive measures against those breaking trust in violation of regulations, according to the gravity of the circumstances, both for corporate members and individual members.

Promote the creation of socialized constraint and punishment. Perfect social public opinion supervision mechanisms, strengthen disclosure and exposure of trust-breaking acts, give rein to the role of the masses in appraisal, discussion, criticism and reports, shape social deterrence through social moral condemnation, and censure trust-breaking acts of members of society.

Establish rewarded reporting systems for" (a rewards system for reporting) "acts of breach of trust. Realistically implement rewards for reporting individuals, and protect the lawful rights and interests of reporting individuals.

Establish joint credit reward and punishment mechanisms across multiple departments and regions. Through credit information exchange and sharing, realize credit reward alliances across multiple departments and regions; ensure that those keeping trust receive benefit in all respect, and those breaking trust meet with difficulty at every step.

2) Establishing and completing legal, regulatory and standards systems for credit.

Perfect legal and regulatory systems for credit. Move credit legislation forward, ensure there are laws to rely on for credit information collection, consulting, use, exchange and interaction, credit information security, the protection of subjects' rights and interests, etc. Publish supplementary rules and implementation regulations for the 'Credit Investigation Management Regulations', establish systems to process objections, handle complaints and punish liability for infringement.

Move forward the construction of sectoral, departmental and local credit structures. All localities and all departments must, according to the needs of sectoral credit system construction within their own localities and departments, formulate regulatory structures for regional or sectoral credit construction, clarify the responsibilities of credit information recording subjects, guarantee the objectivity, truthfulness, accuracy and timely updating of credit information, perfect credit information sharing and openness systems, promote the orderly development and use of credit information resources.

Establish categorized credit information management systems. Formulate credit information catalogues, determine the categories of credit information, according to the attributes of credit information, and in integration with the protection of personal privacy and commercial secrets, move categorized management of credit information forward according to the law, in segments such as collection, sharing, use openness, etc. Enhance investigation and prosecution of the sale of personal privacy and commercial secrets.

Accelerate the construction of credit information standard systems. Formulate nationwide uniform credit information collection and categorized management standards, and unify the credit indicator catalogue and construction standards.

Establish uniform social credit coding systems. Establish uniform social credit coding systems for natural persons, legal persons and other organizations. Perfect corresponding structures and standards, and promote the broad use of uniform social credit codes in economic and social activities.

3) Foster and standardize credit service markets.

Develop various kinds of credit service structures. Progressively establish credit service organization systems where public credit service bodies and social credit service bodies interact and mutually supplement each other, at multiple levels and in all directions in a manner where basic credit information services and value-added services complement each other.

Move forward and standardize the development of a credit rating industry. Foster and develop local rating bodies, and strengthen the international competitiveness of our country's rating bodies. Standardize and develop a credit rating market, raise the overall credibility of the credit rating industry. Explore and innovate double rating and re-rating systems. Encourage our country's rating bodies to participate in international competition and the formulation of international standards, and strengthen coordination and cooperation with credit rating bodies in other countries.

Promote the broad utilization of credit service products. Expand the scope of application of credit service products, and expand the application of credit service products in social governance and market exchange. Encourage credit service product research, development and innovation, and promote the development of credit insurance, credit guarantee, commercial factoring, performance guarantees, credit management consulting and training and other such credit service activities.

Establish orderly and open government credit information systems. Determine the open categories and basic catalogues for governmental credit information, broaden government credit information openness to society in an orderly manner, and optimize the development environment for credit investigation, credit rating, credit management, and other such industries.

Perfect credit service market supervision and management systems. On the basis of the different characteristics of the activities of credit service markets and bodies, implement categorized supervision and management according to the law, perfect supervision and management systems, clarify supervision and management duties and responsibilities, realistically safeguard market order. Promote the formulation of legal systems concerning credit service activities, establish credit service bodies access and withdrawal mechanisms, realize that employment qualification assessment is open and transparent, further perfect professional norms for credit services, and stimulate the healthy development of the credit services sector.

Promote the perfection of legal person governance for credit services bodies. Strengthen internal control in credit service bodies, perfect constraining mechanisms, improve the quality of credit services.

Strengthen the construction of credit for credit service bodies themselves. Credit service bodies must establish behavioural norms, strengthen standards and management, raise service quality, persist in fairness and independence, and raise their credibility. All kinds of credit service bodies are encouraged to set up chief credit supervision officers, and to strengthen their credit management.

Strengthen self-discipline in credit service industries. Promote the establishment of self-disciplinary organizations for the credit service industry, set up behavioural norms and professional standards within organizations for credit service bodies and employees, strengthen self-restraint and comprehensively improve the sincerity levels of credit service bodies.

4) Protect the rights and interests of credit information subjects.

Complete protection mechanisms for the rights and interests of information credit subjects. Fully give rein to the role of administrative supervision, sectoral self-discipline and social supervision in protecting the rights and interests of credit information subjects; comprehensively use legal, economic, administrative and other such measures to realistically protect the rights and interests of credit information subjects. Strengthen guidance and education of credit information subjects, incessantly strengthen their consciousness about upholding their own lawful rights and interests.

Establish self-correction and active self-renewal social incentive and care mechanisms. With establishing educational mechanisms aimed at trust-breaking acts by minors as a focus point, provide appropriate protection to members of society who regret and have corrected past light acts of trust-breaking, and shape incentive mechanisms for trust-keeping and advancement.

Establish credit information infringement liability investigation mechanisms. Formulate management rules and operational regulations for processing objections, handling complaints and managing litigation concerning credit information. Further strengthen law enforcement, and strictly punish the leaking of State secrets or commercial secrets, or the infringement of personal privacy by credit service bodies and other such unlawful acts according to the law. Strengthen the role of social supervision through exposing various kinds of acts violating information subjects' rights and interests through all kinds of media.

5) Strengthen credit information security management.

Complete credit information security management systems. Perfect credit information protection and online trust systems, establish and complete credit information security supervision systems. Strengthen credit information security supervision and inspection, launch credit information security risk assessment, implement hierarchical credit information security protection. Launch credit information security authentication, strengthen credit information security emergency response handling mechanisms. Strengthen credit information security infrastructure construction.

Strengthen credit service bodies' internal credit information security management. Strengthen the ability of credit service bodies to protect security, expand security guarantees, technological research and development and financial input, build credit information security guarantee systems with high starting points and high standards. Formulate and implement regulatory structures for credit information gathering, ordering, processing, storage, usage, and other such areas.

VI) Establishing implementation and support systems

1) Strengthening responsibility and implementation.

All localities and all departments must unify thoughts, and according to the general requirements of this Planning Outline, establish Planning Outline Promotion Small Groups, to formulate concrete implementation plans on the basis of the division of work and responsibility, and the work reality.

All localities and all departments must regularly conduct a summary and evaluation of the situation of the construction of a social credit system in their localities and corresponding sectors, timely discover problems and put forward solutions for improvement.

Localities, departments and work units with prominent achievements in social credit system construction will be commended according to regulations. Responsible personnel within localities, departments and work units that do not move matters forward forcefully or where many acts of untruthfulness occur will be held to administrative accountability according to regulations.

2) Expanding policy support.

All levels' People's Governments must, on the basis of the needs of social credit system construction, bring expenses that should be borne by governments into their financial budget, in order to guarantee them. Expand financial support for the construction of credit infrastructure, innovation and demonstration project in focus areas, etc.

All localities and all departments are encouraged to integrate the deployment of the Planning Outline with their own work reality, take the lead and engage in pioneering trials in the area of social credit system construction innovation and demonstration, and provide support in government budgets, financial arrangements and other such areas.

3) Implementing specific projects.

The Government Affairs Information Openness Project.
Deeply implement the 'Government Information Openness Regulations of the People's Republic of China', conduct categorized management according to the principles of active openness and openness on request; realistically expand the strength of government affairs openness, and establish an open and transparent government image.

The Rural Credit System Construction Project.
Establish credit files for peasant households, farms, peasant cooperatives, the fallow agricultural sector, agricultural production and processing enterprises and other such rural members of society, and ram down a basis for the construction of a rural credit system. Develop credit account, credit village and credit town (township) creation activities, deeply move youth credit demonstration household work forward, give rein to the role of model examples, ensure that peasants receive education and tangible benefits through participation, and raise their credit awareness through practice. Move forward with the construction of credit construction in agricultural product production, processing and distribution enterprises, the fallow agricultural sector and other such agriculture-related enterprises. Establish and complete mutual peasant credit guarantee systems, move forward and develop rural insurances, perfect village credit guarantee systems.

The Small and Micro-Enterprise Credit System Construction Project.
Establish and complete credit recording and evaluation systems suited to the characteristics of small and micro-enterprises. Perfect credit information consulting and sharing service networks for small and micro-enterprises, and regional small and micro-enterprise credit records. Guide all kinds of credit service organs to provide information services to small and micro-enterprises, innovate concentrated credit service methods for small and micro-enterprises, encourage the creation of varied sincerity propaganda and

training activities for small and micro-enterprises, create a good credit environment for small and micro-enterprises to raise funds, and for their healthy development.

4) Promoting examples of innovation.

Comprehensive demonstrations of local credit construction.
Demonstration regions are to take the lead in integrating credit information in all local departments and work units, creating uniform credit information sharing platforms, and open these up to society in an orderly manner and according to the law. All departments in demonstration regions are to strengthen the use of credit information and credit products in the process of carrying out economic and social management, and providing public services, and are to provide essential conditions for punishment management and service.

Establish and complete social credit reward and punishment mechanisms, and ensure that those keeping trust are incentivized and rewarded, and those breaking trust are restrained and sanctioned. Publicize model acts of trust-breaking violating laws and regulations, and strengthen the attack against grave acts of trust-breaking. Explore the establishment of local government credit evaluation standards and methods, and try out local government comprehensive credit evaluation in issuing local government bonds and other such credit and finance activities conforming to the provisions of laws and regulations.

Cooperative demonstrations of regional credit construction.
Explore the establishment of regional interlinked credit mechanisms, carry out regional credit system construction and innovation trials, move forward with credit information exchange and sharing, realize interregional credit rewards and punishments, and optimize the regional credit environment.

Applied credit information demonstrations in focus areas and sectors.
Try out the implementation of the credit reporting system in food security, environmental protection, production safety, product quality, project construction, e-commerce, negotiable securities and futures, funding guarantees, government procurement, tendering and bidding and other such areas.

5) Complete organizational guarantees.

Perfect organizational coordinating mechanisms. Perfect interministerial joint conference systems for the construction of the social credit system. Fully give rein to its coordinating and planning role, strengthen guidance, supervision and inspection of the work of all localities and all departments, in constructing a social credit system. Establish nationwide credit associations, strengthen sectoral self-discipline, and fully give rein to the role of all kinds of social organizations in moving forward the construction of a social credit system.

Build local government promotion mechanisms. All levels' local People's Governments must put the construction of a social credit system on the important matters agenda, move forward the construction of government affairs sincerity, commercial sincerity, social sincerity and judicial credibility; strengthen supervision, strengthen assessment, and make the construction of a social credit system into an important element of assessing work objectives and tasks, and evaluating officials' career achievements.

Establish work reporting and coordination systems. The interministerial joint conference for the construction of a social credit system is to regularly convene work coordination meetings, report the situation of work progress, and timely research and resolve major problems in the construction of a social credit system.

Posted on June 14, 2014
Updated on April 25, 2015
State Council Notice concerning Issuance of the
Planning Outline for the Construction of a Social Credit System (2014-2020)
GF No. (2014)21

All provincial, autonomous region and municipal People's Governments, all State Council ministries and commissions, all directly subordinate departments.

The 'Planning Outline for the Construction of a Social Credit System (2014-2020)' is hereby issued to you. Please implement it earnestly. State Council, 14 June 2014

(This document is for public circulation)

What follows are two important studies about the now-ongoing rollout of China's Social Credit System, done by the Mercator Institute for China Studies (www.merics.org) in Berlin, Germany, as part of its China Monitor.

The first (www.merics.org/en/china-monitor/content/518) is entitled "China's Social Credit System", subtitled, "A Big Data Approach to Market Regulation With Broad Implications For Doing Business In China", is written Mirjam Meissner, and dated May 24, 2017.

The study/article begins with the following **Summary**:

"China's Social Credit System introduces a novel big data-enabled toolkit for monitoring, rating and steering the behavior of market participants in a more comprehensive manner than existing credit rating mechanisms. If implemented successfully, the system will strengthen the Chinese government's capacity to enforce and fine tune market regulations and industrial policies in a sophisticated manner.

As a showcase of 'top-level design' under central coordination, implementation of the Social Credit System is progressing fast. Over the past two years, major hubs have been established for data collection and sharing. Various government entities and commercial credit rating services have begun processing and evaluating the data provided. In spite of many bureaucratic and technology barriers, the basic structures of the system are planned to be in place by 2020.

The ultimate goal is to build self-enforcing mechanisms for business regulation: Based on advanced big data technologies, the system is designed to constantly monitor and evaluate companies' economic as well as non-economic behavior. Automatically generated and updated rating scores will have an immediate impact on their business opportunities. Intervention by government bodies can thus be reduced to setting the rules, standards, and eventually, algorithms for the system. This will minimize their constant supervision of and visible interference in market processes.

The system will create strong incentives for companies to make their business decisions and operations comply not just with laws and regulations but also with the industrial and technological policy targets laid down by the Chinese government. Foreign companies active in the Chinese market are planned to be integrated into the system and treated the same way as their Chinese competitors. Foreign companies will also be subjected to the full extent of industrial policy guidance.

At the heart of the Social Credit System lies massive data collection on company activities by government agencies and authorized rating entities. The system has the potential to strengthen the transparency and trustworthiness in market exchanges as well as the socially and environmentally responsible behavior of companies. On the other hand it will be prone to failing technologies, data manipulation, and the politically induced, unidirectional allocation of investments. It will thus reduce the capacity for autonomous business decisions or non-standard disruptive models and pose a constant risk to the protection of proprietary company data.

Companies should take the accelerating implementation of the system and its impact on doing business in and with China very seriously. Companies need to proactively examine the specific plans and their foreseeable impact on their respective business sectors. Economic diplomacy and business associations will have to consider how they can try to co-shape the implementation of the new rating system and contain its potential risks.

The Aim

Introducing Novel Tools For Monitoring And Regulating Market behavior

Under the catchphrase 'Social Credit System', China is currently implementing a new and highly innovative approach to monitoring, rating, and regulating the behavior of market participants. The Social Credit System will have significant impact on the behavior of individuals, companies, and other institutions, such as NGOs. Despite much international attention on the impact of the systems for individuals, the core motivation behind the Social Credit System is to more effectively steer the behavior of market participants.

The Social Credit System goes far beyond credit rating systems in Europe or the U.S.: it expands the use of credit ratings to the social, environmental, and political realm. Under China's Social Credit System, a company will get a lower credit rating if it does not pay its loans back in time. It will, however, also get a lower rating if it does not comply with emissions targets, work safety standards, or government investment requirements, or if it fails to deliver products ordered via e-commerce platforms on time. Possible punishments as a result of bad ratings include:

Unfavorable conditions for a new loan
Higher taxes than compliant competitors
No permission to issue any bonds or invest in companies listed on the stock market
Decreased chances to participate in publicly funded projects
Mandatory government approval for investments, even in sectors where market access is not usually regulated

In severe cases, the company's e-commerce accounts could be shut down and even its high-level management's individual credit ratings could be affected. A company's manager could be denied tickets for high-speed trains or for international business flights. On the other hand, a fully compliant company can benefit from:

A largely open Chinese market with manifold investment opportunities
Low tax burdens
Good credit conditions
Gentle support from government incentive mechanisms

A) The core concept: self-restriction of companies

If the Chinese government succeeds in implementing the Social Credit System and its related mechanisms, companies' market activities will be regulated in a self-enforcing manner: Enabled by advanced big data technologies, the system is designed to constantly monitor and evaluate companies' economic as well as non-economic behavior. Automatically generated and updated rating scores will have an immediate impact on companies' business opportunities. This creates a strong incentive for companies to make their business decisions and operations comply not just with laws and regulations but also with government's industrial and technological policy targets. Beijing terms this the 'self-restriction of companies'.

B) The essence: massive data collection

The essence of the Social Credit System is to amass a huge collection of data on companies which will be used to generate ratings for each company. The government's aim is to include general information on companies, information on their compliance with government regulations and wherever practical, real-time data on their behavior. Eventually, the Social Credit System is supposed to integrate central and local government data, data from industry associations as well as data from commercial rating services. The data will be collected on a platform overseen by the central government.

Considering the extraordinary speed of digitization in China, the future potential for data collection via real-time monitoring is almost unlimited: E-commerce platforms could provide the Social Security System with data on companies' reliability during online business activities, for example, with regard to payments, delivery product quality, and customer satisfaction. Particularly for companies active in the automobile, transportation, and logistics industries, real-time monitoring of cars via traffic systems and on-board units will provide the basis for their future social credit ratings. This could include not only data on the behavior of professional drivers, but also data on emissions and the technical performance of a car.

For polluting industries, the government's goal is to measure environmental compliance with real-time emissions data, from sensor systems in chimney stacks, and real-time energy consumption, with the help of smart meters.

A considerable number of pilot projects have already been launched to test the employment of real-time monitoring systems. If they are successfully put into practice, the Social Credit System will allow for immediate and automated responses to misbehavior of companies: A lower social credit rating and related punishments could follow within seconds after a major payment default in e-commerce trade, a sudden increase in energy use beyond a permitted level, or after a certain number of traffic fines for the drivers of a transport company.

C) The generation of social credit scores: a decentralized process

As it stands, the Social Credit System will not generate one single score for every company. Instead, the government plans suggest a rather diversified and decentralized market for social credit ratings. This includes central government credit records focusing on major offenses, sectoral social credit ratings, commercial credit rating services, as well as the People's Bank of China's credit rating center. However many questions remain open with regard to the exact future shape of the system's rating mechanisms. A centralization of social credit ratings, as soon as the necessary technical solutions are sufficiently developed, cannot be ruled out.

D) The impact of social credit scores: influencing business opportunities

The central government plans and the implementation guidelines by ministries provide detailed lists on the possible impact of social credit ratings on businesses." A more complete list of possible benefits could include:

"Subsidies
Issuing of bonds
Access to public procurement: public-private partnerships,
   government pilot projects, public service projects
Governmental land distribution
Credit conditions
Intensity of government monitoring
Investment opportunities
Access to online retail platforms/social media
Travel privileges
Career opportunities

Eventually, the move of the Chinese government towards more open markets and less intrusive state intervention is counterbalanced by the Social Credit System. One prominent example is the introduction of negative lists which will replace China's investment catalogues and reduce the number of industries where government approval is required for foreign investments. However, only companies with clean social credit records are to benefit from this reduction of state regulation. The Social Credit System is to make sure that companies not fully complying with government rules have significantly lower investment opportunities on the Chinese market and cannot freely conduct their business in unrestricted sectors. Some of the recently established free trade zones (FTZ) will serve as testing grounds for linking investment opportunities and social credit ratings.

E) The scope: covering the whole economy

From an international perspective, it is important to note that government documents referring to the Social Credit System do not discriminate between Chinese and foreign businesses. The same is true for private and state-owned enterprises. Implementation will show whether this principle will remained unchanged. It is, however, likely that foreign businesses active on the Chinese market will be fully integrated into the system and treated the same way as their Chinese competitors. Simultaneously, foreign companies will be subjected to the full extent of industrial policy guidance.

Generally, China's Social Credit System is designed to cover the whole economy. At this initial stage, though, released government plans focus on key sectors that are either identified as industries of strategic importance for future economic development (e.g. the automobile industry) or for the stable provision of infrastructure and basic service, including the telecommunications, energy and food industries. A particularly strong focus is on e-commerce. All these key industries will feel the impact of the system soon. An expansion to other industries is to be expected in the foreseeable future.

The Process

A) The process: fast implementation of a mammoth project

The implementation of China's Social Credit System faces two major obstacles: bureaucratic barriers and technological feasibility. Nevertheless, compared to other projects and reforms prioritized under the leadership of Xi Jinping and Li Keqiang, the Social Credit System is by far one of the most dynamic and fast-moving.

The project has been prepared over a long period of time: In the late 1990s, Lin Junyue's working group at the Institute of World Economics and Politics of the Chinese Academy of Sciences developed the basic concepts and mechanisms of the system. Lin himself is often referred to as the pioneer of the 'Theory of the Social Credit System'. He was educated and started his career in the U.S. as an expert on information retrieval and credit ratings. Based on these experiences, Lin and his colleagues advocated a unique Chinese approach to credit ratings. Numerous pilot projects were already started in the early 2000s.

B) Dynamic start: concerted action under top leadership supervision

As a showcase of 'top level design' under central coordination, implementation has been progressing quickly since the release of the central government's 'Plan for Establishing a Social Credit System' in 2014. The schedule for implementation is tight: Beijing wants to have the system up and running by 2020. The project is coordinated by the influential Central Leading Small Group for Comprehensively Deepening Reforms, headed by party and state leader Xi himself. The Leading Small group has assigned the National Development and Reform Commission (NDRC) to lead the implementation process in close cooperation with the People's Bank of China (PBOC). Since August 2015, both have authorized a total number of 43 pilot cities and city districts to implement the Social Credit System and experiment with related mechanisms. Another testing ground is the afore-mentioned Free Trade Zones (FTZs).

C) Work in progress: establishing a hub for sharing and collecting data

The data backbone of the Social Credit System is the so-called 'National Credit Information Sharing Platform'. The platform has been up and running since October 2015. Its purpose is to collect and share data from local and central governments, from sectoral Social Credit Systems and also, in the future, from commercial credit rating companies. During the past two years (2015-2017), visible progress has been made with regard to the integration of data from multiple sources on the National Sharing Platform.

Currently, the platform collects mainly government data and includes a total number of 400 databases by more than 30 central ministries and governmental agencies, who rely on the input of provincial and city-level government data. More than 80% of the integrated data covers information on companies – with most data being supplied by the two ministries responsible for economic development, namely the NDRC and the Ministry of Industry and Information Technology (MIIT). As of today (note: likely May 2017), approximately 75% of the government data collected in the Sharing Platform is publicly available and, in case of company data, accessible to a significant extent online via the National Enterprise Credit Information Publicity System. Only 25% is qualified as data for limited sharing or inter-government sharing. From a technical perspective, the sharing platform can be searched by a company's name as well as by a company's Social Credit Number.

As of 2016, the company-related information collected on the National Credit Information Sharing Platform included general data on companies, like registered capital, legal representatives, investment activities, annual reports, government-approved projects, criminal records and the like. Additionally, it integrates a broad set of data on companies' compliance with government regulations as well as data concerning public welfare and security, like information on product safety, environmental protection, and work safety. Furthermore, it includes information on unfair business practices, like intellectual property rights violations or tax fraud. The list of integrated data also reveals that much of the collected data is presumably still paper-based and relies on face-to-face inspections by government agencies. Much still needs to be done if the government wants to automate data collection and integrate real-time monitoring systems.

D) Data evaluation: multiple rating services involved

While many details on the collection and sharing of data under the Social Credit System are available, systematic information on the use and evaluation of the collected data is rare. As mentioned, the Social Credit System will presumably not generate one single credit score for every company. Instead, several rating systems with varying assessment criteria currently exist in parallel, to be employed for different purposes. The exact algorithms and criteria generating the different credit ratings remain unknown.

Several different entities will process the company data collected by the Social Credit System, evaluate them, and generate social credit ratings. They include the two government credit information platforms, the National Enterprise Credit Information Publicity System and the Credit China Platform, as well as the Credit Reference Centre of the PBOC, commercial credit rating services, and sectoral credit rating systems. The main characteristics of these social credit rating entities are as follows:

The government credit information platforms, the National Enterprise Credit Information Publicity System, and the Credit China Platform provide information on blacklisted companies as well as an overview of companies' positive and negative credit records. The implementation is still far from a sophisticated approach to credit ratings, but rather a simple register of a company's positive and negative records. Existing blacklists include, for example, lists of thousands of companies not allowed to issue bonds or to invest in publicly traded companies. Ministries and other government agencies are supposed to use the available information during approval or bidding processes.

The Credit Reference Center of the PBOC, established in 2004, is supposed to become an important credit rating authority under the Social Credit System. The center's Financial Credit Information Database is a main provider for the Social Credit System and might also use data from the National Credit Information Sharing Platform to generate its company credit scores. The PBOC ratings are already being used by government agencies in bidding processes and other administrative decisions. It can be expected that the Credit Reference Center, or a newly created rating center under the PBOC, will take a vital role in rating companies under the Social Credit System in the future.

Commercial credit rating services are a substantial part of the Social Credit System. The idea of the government is to share its own data with these commercial services and to receive their data on companies' trustworthiness in return. A broad mix of companies are currently accessing the market with their own company rating services, including Alibaba and JD (major e-commerce companies), Baidu (China's Google), Wanda (commercial property company and cinema chain operator) as well as China Telecom (state-owned telecommunication company), Fosun (investment company) and some ministry-backed rating companies. As of March 2017, 137 commercial credit reporting companies were active on the Chinese market, most based in Beijing or Shanghai. Whether data exchange between these companies and the National Credit Information Sharing Platform already exists, remains an open question for the time being. Some companies reportedly signed contracts for sharing credit information with the state's data platform.

In focus industries targeted by the Social Credit System, industry associations or ministries currently work on the implementation of sectoral credit rating systems. This includes the automotive, energy, finance, and e-commerce industries. The ratings generated by these sectoral systems will presumably be integrated into the National Credit Information Sharing Platform.

E) Moving ahead: smooth implementation is unlikely

One of the key challenges of the Social Credit System's implementation is the systemic integration of data collected by private companies. The project's success depends heavily on their willingness to share their data and on the government's capacity to enforce data sharing. The business case might be attractive in some cases due to the possibility of gaining access to government data. On the other hand, companies like Alibaba, JD, or Baidu might refuse to share their proprietary data, as it is their most valuable product." (Note: "refuse" seems like a strong word to be using in this instance – does any company, no matter how big, have the "ability" to refuse China's central government's "request" for such actions?!)

"Technological obstacles also remain high: database infrastructure and the ability of the various government and commercial systems to enhance data quality and to evaluate massive amounts of real-time data pose huge challenges for implementation. Compared to many other countries, China is well prepared to overcome those challenges. It does not only have the political will and assertiveness but also the financial resources, and it is already strong in decisive technologies, such as big data or surveillance systems.

Bureaucratic processes may also hamper progress. Reliable data provision by province and city-level governments as well as by companies is not a matter of course. There is likely to be resistance when it comes to handing over data. And even real-time monitoring systems are not safe from data fraud: a recent case of real-time emissions data being faked by companies shows that China still has a long way to go to building a reliable base for the Social Credit System.

The Social Credit System will presumably not show its full potential impact on companies by 2020. However, the government's commitment to the project is unquestionable. China will invest all efforts into implementing the basic structure and mechanisms as soon as possible.

The Consequences

A new type of big data-enabled market regulation

If implemented as proposed, the Social Credit System has the potential to help solve many pressing issues in the Chinese economy. It will, however, also facilitate an IT-backed authoritarianism: the Chinese government's capacity to enforce and fine tune its market regulations and industrial policies will be enhanced through new incentive mechanisms – the credit scores generated by the Social Credit System – thereby establishing a subtle," (? Note – is there anything subtle about such a system; "should" there be anything subtle about such a system; is there any intention that such a system should be at all subtle?) "self-enforcing, and invisible (? Note again – to the contrary, I'm not so sure it's intended to be all that invisible, in the sense that it's going to be ubiquitous, all-encompassing; and therefore always running quietly in the background, as a known and accepted fact of life!) "type of state control. Intervention by government bodies can be reduced to setting the rules, standards, and algorithms for the system, while minimizing constant supervision and interference in the implementation process.

In economic terms, the Social Credit System helps China to internalize political, social and environmental externalities deep into daily business decisions. While many of the relevant regulations are not new to the Chinese market, the Social Credit System brings their enforcement to a new level, by linking them directly to a company's cost-benefit calculation and future business opportunities.

Eventually, the Social Credit System could become a powerful, big data-enabled toolkit for monitoring, rating and steering the behavior of market participants into a politically desired direction: if companies not fulfilling industrial investment targets for a new technology are punished with bad social credit records (as is currently underway for the e-car quota), they will feel pressured to comply with political targets and pour money into technologies that they would – from a purely business-oriented perspective – not consider a profitable investment." And note: a "free market" system has its way of effectively doing the same thing – government-backed defense-oriented and health-oriented centrally/federally funded research and development that provides the necessary incentive for companies and researchers to get involved in projects that might not be short-term attractive, promising, or profitable! So the exact means may be different more superficially, but the goals, and often the results, can be quite comparable. In the West it is more a function of a perhaps less visible government-military-industrial complex working very closely together, while in China it appears to be a much more visible and strongly-led government effort!

"Chinese leadership is convinced of its ability to guide China's economy on a long-term path towards becoming an industrial superpower. If China's comprehensive industrial policies and state-guided investment pattern prove to have the desired effects, the Social Credit System will be a powerful instrument in realizing China's ambitions. However, as is the case for any industrial or technological policy, politically-induced investments may also lead to a massive misallocation of resources, narrowing the space for autonomous business decisions or non-standard (disruptive) business models. Severe economic damage could be the result. These risks are not deterring the Chinese government, however, from determinedly building a sophisticated enforcement mechanism for its industrial policies."

Note: there's denying that! On the other hand, it could prove to be an efficient and effective way to ensure that society's most important needs are really met – if somehow, some way, the will to act with more of the society's and people's needs are kept firmer in mind, by the people themselves, by "business" people, by government officials from the highest to the lowest rankings, and the people's leaders! But the reality: no matter the system of government, and the system of doing business, and the actions of the people themselves, unless everyone shares the vision of how everyone benefits from more egalitarian and mutually-beneficial actions, then this just won't be the way things are!

"A) Potential positive impact: responsible behavior of companies

Apart from these fundamental questions, China's Social Credit System may well have very concrete positive effects on the Chinese economy, if fully implanted as planned:

The Social Credit System could prevent illegal behavior, help strengthen companies' economic trustworthiness, and contribute to building up a new culture of socially and environmentally responsible behavior.

Making comprehensive information on companies and their social credit records accessible for everyone on centralized platforms can increase transparency on companies' activities. The social credit records and scores, for example, help businesses to better judge a potential partner or acquisition target.

Concurrently to the implementation of the system, China will try to significantly enhance the quality of collected data. This can have a positive impact on the reliability of existing economic statistics, if used accordingly.

The Social Credit System and its vast database create a big, new playing field for companies specializing in big data. Real-time monitoring systems create new markets for advanced IT-technologies, ranging from traffic monitoring and image recognition to satellite navigation systems. Positive effects on China's technological development and abilities are likely, and could turn China into the leading, global market for these technologies.

B) Potential negative impact: risking economic damage

The Social Credit System will also yield substantial negative impacts. Possible examples are:

A considerable number of companies might not be able to carry the costs of compliance with the government's regulations. For example, in the case of adhering to environmental standards during production. Since non-compliance will not be an option with the Social Credit System at work, some might be forced to close their business or restrict investments." Note – of course this has both a negative and positive impact, since environmentally the end result is that the people of China are much better off if the environment is thus more protected, rather than less so!

"Particularly during the implementation process, China's Social Credit System will very likely be prone to error, due to immature technologies. Compliant companies might get bad ratings and vice-versa, which will inevitably cause economic damage.

The Social Credit System may pose a constant risk to the protection of proprietary company data. A major data leak or theft could easily result in severe economic damage through the sharing or selling of sensitive company data to competitors or other states.

Compared to other countries, the Chinese government has much more leeway in collecting and using data. A fundamental problem of the system could be the misuse of proprietary data by Chinese government entities, which could be highly damaging to companies' business.

While public access to information creates transparency, the algorithms of the various credit rating services in calculating credit scores remain opaque. Their increasing importance can make business activities in China highly unpredictable.

C) Potential international impact: new challenges for international companies

To international stakeholders, the Social Credit System poses significant challenges: It is highly likely that international companies will be fully integrated into the Social Credit System's mechanisms. If they comprehensively comply with government regulations, they can avoid painful punishments, but their freedom of business decision-making in China will be significantly constrained. International companies might, like their Chinese competitors, for example, be forced to make economically unreasonable investments, stipulated by China's industrial policy guidance."

Note – or more likely to be the case, international businesses who want to stay in China will find a way to make it into just another cost of doing business in China, the same way they've been finding a way of doing things for a long time now! And then those extra costs will be a burden for the consumer, but hopefully the consumer will be shown that those extra costs come with clearly demonstrable benefits as well!

"At the same time, the integration of international companies could actually create a more level playing field between international companies and their Chinese competitors, since both are subject to the same social credit rating mechanisms influencing their business opportunities. However, it remains questionable as to whether this will lead to significantly less discrimination of international companies in practice, for example, during public bidding processes. In fact, the social credit ratings might just as well turn out to become an additional, and very subtle, tool for discrimination. Ratings for international companies could easily be subject to systematic and intentional bias in favor of Chinese enterprises." Note – if that does indeed prove to be the case, then it will be more as political decision as much as an economic one – where central authorities decide that international companies' role in Chinese society should play a clearly subordinate role to domestic companies; and that if international companies object, they're free to pull up stakes in China and leave!

"On top of that, data security concerns will increasingly impact international companies' business in China. This relates not only to the risk of data theft, but also to the potential misuse of sensitive data by government agencies. The sensitive technical data of high-tech companies could be at particular risk if China introduces real-time monitoring systems collecting technical data. An example is on-board units in cars, monitoring not only the behavior of the driver but also the technical performance of the car itself." Note – this is indeed a real, and very serious, problem! But, in reality, has little to do with the Social Credit System, and more with Chinese political and governmental decisions, about the necessity and desirability of protecting foreign intellectual property on many levels. In particular, the stipulated sharing of highly technical and innovative knowledge and data with a domestic business partner is an explosive issue in and of itself, let alone in the context of a social credit system!

"Ultimately, China's Social Credit System could fast become a global phenomenon: Related IT-systems and big data solutions have high export potential to countries where the goal of strengthening state control of the economy is prominent. While implementation will always require a certain level of bureaucratic and technological capability, China's approach to the regulation of the economy could become a role model for other economies worldwide, if the Social Credit System proves to be successful.

Companies active in the Chinese market should take the speedy implementation of the system very seriously, as the development will impact their business in and with China. They urgently need to develop a deeper understanding of the Social Credit System's conception and mechanisms, if they do not want to be caught on the back foot when the system takes effect. Regulatory specifications and rating platforms are currently taking shape. Companies need to proactively examine the specific plans and foreseeable impact in their respective business sectors. Economic diplomacy and business associations, also in coordination with Chinese enterprises, will have to consider how they can try to shape the implementation of the new rating system and contain the potential risks.

Conclusion

Evolvement of a highly competitive economic system?

The Social Credit System embodies China's vision to create a highly effective and, at the same time, adaptive economy under political leadership. If implemented as planned, the system has the potential to become the most globally sophisticated and fine-tuned model for IT-backed and big data-enabled market regulation. It would deeply transform the Chinese economy and provide China's policymakers with a tool to effectively and rapidly react to upcoming social and environmental challenges as well as to new technologies and industrial developments. China's government will attempt to use the Social Credit System to channel investment into cutting-edge technologies and to steer companies into patterns of behavior useful in solving social and environmental problems. This could, in turn, accelerate leapfrogging processes, innovative business activities, and the Chinese society's ability to quickly adapt to unforeseen changes. In this case, Western market economies, in comparison, would appear slow-moving and highly fragmented, with a weak capacity for implementation and lacking in long-term strategy. In the vision of China's leadership, liberal market economies would ultimately not be able to compete with the Chinese unidirectional approach." And, unfortunately, political and leadership, as well as serious economic, issues, now running rampant through Western market economies, make it even less likely that they will be able to strongly stand up to and compete with such highly determined and focused efforts now driving China's political and economic efforts!

And this study/article ends with: "Yet China's vision of comprehensively steering economic activities is very ambitious. The project will not necessarily be crowned with success. Given its limitations and weaknesses, the Social Credit System might just as easily result in a massive decline in investments, the failure of whole industries, low innovative power and little entrepreneurial initiative. Whether or not the Chinese approach will prove to be better suited to the technological, social and environmental challenges of the 21st century remains an open question. It is certain, however, that the Chinese leadership is fully committed to investing everything necessary in order for its mammoth Social Credit System to succeed."

And I add: should this effort end with this "massive decline in investments, the failure of whole industries, low innovative power and little entrepreneurial initiative", it would be an unmitigated disaster for China and the entire world. Nevertheless, sometimes it can seem like the world is already on the edge of an economic and social abyss; and retrogressive and highly negatively-oriented American "leadership" is certainly not helping the situation. So it would appear, that if anyone at this time has the necessary financial, political, economic and social resources and resolve to at least point some kind of way forward, it just might well be China and its Social Credit System, even if its methods might seem alien, even distasteful, to Western thought and ways of going about doing things! There's a lot that's positive, as well as negative, in the Chinese way of going about doing things, even if in the end they don't prove to be very successful in their efforts. As the world is getting smaller, it is absolutely necessary that we learn from each other – and learn to live with each other. The Chinese Social Credit System that is in serious development has a lot to teach about possible ways we can live together, as well as traps that could easily be fallen into, in the hands of people and leaders whose own interests are far different than those of the people they ultimately are responsible for, and ideally, report to! Bringing things out in the open is the best way to make sure leaders, government and people's interests are strongly aligned! That's why so much more needs to be told and known about this Chinese effort!

The second study/article that will be examined closely, that also came out of the Mercator Institute for China Studies (merics.org), is titled "Central Planning, Local Experiments" and subtitled "The Complex Implementation of China's Social Credit System". It was written by Mareike Ohlberg, Shazeda Ahmed and Bertram Lang, and is dated December 12, 2017 – about a half year later than the first study/article that was examined.

Much like the previously reviewed article, this one begins with a summary, in this instance called "Main Findings And Conclusions:

China's Social Credit System is an ambitious, information technology-driven initiative through which the state seeks to create a central repository of data on natural and legal persons that can be used to monitor, assess, and change their actions through incentives of punishment and reward.

The Chinese government presents the Social Credit System as a cure-all solution to a multitude of disparate societal and economic problems such as the lack of options to assess the financial creditworthiness of market participants, food security and insufficient protection of intellectual property rights.

Neither party-state nor private media fundamentally question the need for the Social Credit System. Social media coverage suggests that many citizens have yet to grasp what the Social Credit System is and what its implications in their daily lives may be.

Even if the full vision of the system is not realized, the scope of this project is massive and will transform China's legal, social, and economic environment significantly.

Several social credit pilot projects are already operational, testing new approaches of collecting data and using it to sanction undesirable behavior on a limited scale. These punishments offer unprecedented possibilities to surveil and steer the behavior of natural and legal persons and therefore would have far-reaching consequences if adopted nationwide.

National implementation is still at an early stage: many of the measures put in place are establishing foundations for sharing information between different departments of government.

Media discussions of the information security and data privacy risks the system poses indicate a lack of consensus on how these issues will be regulated at the provincial and national levels.

The relationship between government and commercial actors will be a key factor to watch: Government agencies clearly depend on private companies' technological know-how to roll out such a large-scale system. Conflicts and rivalry between bureaucratic and commercial players, however, could delay or even derail its implementation.

A Versatile Tool For Steering Behavior:
Understanding China's Social Credit System

In 2014, the Chinese government announced detailed plans to create a Social Credit System that is meant to reward behavior the government considers financially, economically, and socially responsible while also sanctioning non-compliance with its policies. Although the system is inspired by financial credit scoring systems in other countries, it surpasses these in at least three ways:

1) the broader scope of which criteria are evaluated for credit rating purposes,

2) the spectrum and efficient enforcement of punishments and restrictions imposed as a result of non-compliant behavior,

3) the growing use of digital sensors and devices that can continually collect and assess behavioral data in real time.

In the financial sector, credit scoring systems usually reduce transaction costs for loans or online payment services and hold market participants accountable to rules and regulations. However the scope of the Chinese Social Credit System is by no means limited to financial measures of creditworthiness. The aim is to create a central repository of information on natural and legal persons that the state can use to monitor, assess, and ultimately change their actions through behavioral nudges using incentives of punishment and reward. It is based on a combination of traditional sources of data such as financial, criminal, and government records, along with digital sources indicating data collected by Internet of Things-enabled sensors and personal information that individuals provide to websites and mobile phone applications.

Years of social credit policy planning and refinement signify that the Chinese government has embarked on a path-breaking course to comprehensively regulate, rate, and steer the behavior of individuals and companies. As currently envisioned, it is a wide-reaching project that touches on almost all aspects of everyday life. Social credit scoring will not only affect Chinese citizens and companies but will likely also impact foreigners living and working in China as well as have consequences for foreign companies operating in the country. In addition, the provision of social credit scoring services from commercial players such as Alibaba and Tencent, who are simultaneously expanding their global reach, raises questions regarding the extent to which the Social Credit System will collect and use data generated outside of China's borders. Finally, if considered successful, China's Social Credit System may eventually even become a model for other countries in the future.

Despite the anticipated pervasive social and economic impacts, many open questions remain regarding the scope of the system and how it will function when completed. This uncertainty poses a challenge to taking the necessary steps to adapt to the new environment the system will create in China. Individual iterations of the system are currently in the pilot testing phase and are either run by provincial or city governments, or by private companies hailing from the information technology, credit and insurance sectors. One prominent example is Sesame Credit, a non-mandatory credit scoring pilot run by Alibaba's spin-off company Ant Financial Services Group. While the private schemes are more publicly visible and form an important aspect of the broader Social Credit System, the Chinese government's plans cover much more ground.

In order to offer insight into what this system may look like in the future and provide a basis for adapting to it, this study examines the current state of implementation in two steps. First, it will analyze the vision behind the Social Credit System as it is presented in official media as well as how it is discussed in news media and social media in China. Systematic examinations of the range of views that Chinese regulators, scholars, and citizens have expressed regarding the Social Credit System are still largely absent from both domestic and foreign analyses of this new development. Secondly, this study will offer an assessment of the actual state of implementation of the system as of late 2017 based on policy documents, official government websites, reports, and concrete examples of how the Social Credit System is currently being put into action.

By analyzing both what is currently happening on the ground and how Chinese news and social media sources talk about it, we provide answers to questions of what shape China's Social Credit System may take, and which problems its designers and implementers argue have yet to be solved.

Credit Rating 'Plus': China Goes Much Further Than Other Countries

To understand the overarching vision behind the Social Credit System, the scope of issues the Chinese government hopes to solve with it, as well as the roadblocks identified as remaining unsolved in the implementation process, we analyzed official media discussions of the system occurring in the six-month period from January 1 to June 30, 2017, which we accessed through data-scraping software from the media intelligence company Meltwater.

In addition, we scraped social media such as blogs, forums, and bulletin board services (BBS) for non-official discussions of the Social Credit System. The number of hits for the Social Credit System on social media was low (under 2000 hits for the first half of 2017), and a significant proportion of hits consisted of reposted news articles. One notable exception is the database on how Sesame Credit scores are calculated and user-suggested strategies for how to raise one's score. Regulator- and platform-enforced social media censorship as well as self-censorship cannot be excluded as reasons or at least partial explanations for the low number of posts on this potentially sensitive subject.

However, the existence of a small number of fundamentally critical posts combined with the fact that the overall number, including neutral and affirmative posts, is low suggests that thus far, the Social Credit System is not receiving much attention among Chinese citizens. Social media coverage suggests that many users have yet to grasp what the Social Credit System is and what its implications in their daily lives may be.

A) The Government's View: Social Credit As A Cure-All For Social And Economic Problems

The Chinese government considers the Social Credit System an important tool to steer China's economy and to govern society. In Chinese news media, 'social credit' has become an omnipresent political buzzword used by central and provincial government agencies just as much as by financial institutions or public universities. Media debates strongly confirm that the Social Credit System is not seen as merely a way to assess financial creditworthiness. Rather, it is presented as a future cure-all for China's current social and governance problems and meant to solve a disparate range of long-standing issues including, but not limited to, insufficient ways to assess the creditworthiness of market participants, corruption, fraud, and consumer protection issues. Increasing delegation of compliance auditing tasks to information systems and digital sensors underpins much of the vision of the Social Credit System, and is of a piece with the Chinese government's portrayal of big data-driven technological monitoring as providing objective, irrefutable measures of reality.

By design, China's Social Credit System mixes economic criteria with non-economic behavioral criteria to evaluate individuals, companies, and other organizations. The system's declared goal, according to government documents, is to 'improve the integrity awareness and creditworthiness' of Chinese people and ultimately create a trust-based economy and society. In line with this, policy plans focus both on financial credit information on the one hand and integrity, or trustworthiness on a moral level on the other, though occasionally the two are not explicitly differentiated from one another.

While financial credit does factor into the system and the government wants to create a professional, world-class credit service industry, it is mentioned much less frequently both in government plans and in media reports than moral integrity. The main policy document, the State Council's Plan for Establishing a Social Credit System (2014-2020), along with subsequent provincial and sectoral policy plans, distinguish between four 'key areas' for building integrity: government, commerce, society, and legal institutions. Government officials, private individuals, companies, and other legal entities are all to be held accountable for their conduct. In addition, 'creating confidence in the law' is presented as a precondition for creating a functioning Social Credit System in the other domains.

B) Favorable News Media Reports:
Boosting Trust and Integrity Through Technology

China news media most frequently frame social credit as a means of building integrity in society and in government affairs. Integrity in commerce and confidence in the law receive less attention, suggesting that the Social Credit System is presented first and foremost as a tool for governing and reforming society at present.

'Integrity in government affairs' is most often mentioned in conjunction with 'ensuring corruption-free, transparent government' and 'holding government officials accountable' to set an example for other sectors of society. News media often present this as the bedrock principle underlying the engineering of a more trustworthy society. Similarly, 'creating confidence in the law' is presented as a precondition for a functioning credit system in other areas.

In terms of economic governance, the Social Credit System is treated as a catch-all solution for solving market efficiency problems and fighting economic crime. It is regularly mentioned as a solution at the end of articles on various current economic problems, such as product counterfeiting, food and drug safety violations, disrespect of market regulations, etc.

With regards to the societal component, the Social Credit System is regularly associated with the creation of a 'culture of integrity' or the restoration of 'social trust'. The declared goal in official media comments on the system is one of transforming society – which is portrayed as flawed and plagued by untrustworthy elements – for the better.

Among the many problems linked to the diagnosis of a lack of trust in society, food security is commonly identified as the most pressing issue, particularly in private media. Low-quality or contaminated food can severely harm consumers' health. Therefore, unlike for other industries, where consumers' choices will often help eliminate inferior products, market self-regulation does not work here. Instead, as Chinese media argue, 'black sheep' can only be eliminated by building a 'comprehensive Social Credit System.'

The same logic of presenting the Social Credit System as an effort to improve consumer protection in China also underlies the creation of a national-level information platform with explicit reference to the main government plan that promises to 'protect consumers' rights' and provide consumers with 'authoritative' and 'trustworthy' information about goods, manufacturers, and companies.

The analysis of news articles in the first half of 2017 shows that for now, discussions around the Social Credit System remain domestically focused. A possible international extension or even the potential of the Social Credit System to serve as an international model is not mentioned in media articles, in contrast to related domains such as the e-payment sector where China has been recently styling itself as a frontrunner and a model for others to emulate. This supports the view that authorities are not yet confident enough to promote the Social Credit System as an innovative 'Chinese model' of governance. They are far more concerned with making the new system work and legitimizing it domestically at this point.

C) Media Criticism:
Either Constructive or Targeted at Commercial Providers

Neither official nor private media fundamentally question the need for the Social Credit System. While most reporting is neutral or affirmative, some news and social media comments go into more detail to point out problems such as lack of cooperation and disconnected 'data islands' across different bureaucratic entities, self-interest of commercial actors involved in the setting up of the system, inconsistent quality of data collected, lack of uniform data formatting standards, corruption in local government, and even concerns such as privacy infringements and inadequate protection of trade secrets and personal data.

However, criticism is focused on issues that can be technologically solved. It does not question the need for and the legitimacy of the Social Credit System as a means of making moral judgments that will materially affect citizens' social opportunities. Criticism most often concentrates on commercial social credit companies, rather than on the state-run pilots or the system as a whole. In the following section, we introduce some of the points of criticism that are often mentioned in media reports:

Government infrastructure is seen as lagging behind

One commonly mentioned implementation hurdle is insufficient data exchange between different bureaucracies. Media reports have identified lack of cooperation and the subsequent prevalence of 'data islands' as a major problem. The central government presents itself as the most reliable point for collecting information and making sure that all social credit data networks are interconnected and centrally accessible through a single government platform.

However, local government is treated both as part of the problem and of the solution. Corruption in government means that government organs themselves need to be integrated into and evaluated by the Social Credit System. At the same time, all government bureaus are expected to be trailblazers who will be the first to make use of credit information, for instance in public procurement or when deciding who will receive subsidies and preferential policies.

Current types of data collected are deemed inappropriate for assessing creditworthiness

A common concern voiced in news media is that the data privately-run (social) credit providers are collecting is insufficient, inconsistent, or unhelpful for assessing financial creditworthiness. For instance, one article points out that it is not uncommon to find that different commercial credit institutions will use widely diverging ratings to the same person given the disparate data sets and methods drawn upon in evaluation. This problem, according to media reports, is exacerbated by the fact that some government agencies and companies are collecting but not sharing their data with one another, thus creating useless 'data islands.'

Government officials in the banking sector have voiced concern in the media that the mixing of economic and non-economic criteria (as in commercial pilots such as Sesame Credit) is unhelpful in assessing financial credit risks. While the system will still record both types of data, financial regulators have argued that the two need to be clearly separated. Banks may also be wary of the competition that fintech and its related rating and loan-granting systems present, fueling their skepticism of these loosely-regulated alternatives.

There may be ways to cheat the system

By and large, both news and social media are so far avoiding discussions about the potential for cheating or 'gaming' the Social Credit System to artificially produce high scores. There is limited discussion of how to digitally manipulate one's record, how state and private credit score providers will prevent such attempts at fraud, and what the punishments will be for these offenses.

However, one investigative article on Sina Weibo claims that there are data black markets through which Alipay users pay hackers who promise to raise their Sesame Credit scores. Users provide their Alipay usernames and passwords, and the hackers change the 'binding data' that serves to identify users in their profiles, for example upgrading the information to falsely reflect that a user possesses several houses, an expensive car, or a degree from an elite university. The hacker interviewed in the article claims to have made millions in RMB in a few months' time from these orders, even though this method has not been proven to raise Sesame Credit scores by more than a few points. (Note: cited article is titled 'Uncovering The Secret of Sesame Credit: Losers Only Need 400RMB to Become Elite Returnees'; from Sohu.com, and originally dated 10 July 2017.)

This type of fraud poses information security risks given that users cannot guarantee that their Alipay login credentials will not be resold or implicated in identity theft once they have handed them over. As the Social Credit System unfolds, it is likely that additional methods of data forgery will arise.

Commercial providers are criticized for privacy infringements

Considering the troves of highly sensitive personal data the system will collect, information security would presumably be regulators' chief priority. Yet privacy and personal information protection are issues that come up only on the margins in news media, with quotes from government officials and industry representatives describing both as ongoing concerns in establishing a Social Credit System. These are consistently referenced as two separate problems: privacy involves who can access what information about users, and personal information protection relates to the illegal resale of data that could enable blackmail, identity theft, and extortion of social credit users.

News media is critical of private companies having access to too much of citizens' personal data, but to date has not suggested that the government is guilty of this kind of pervasive access. Articles that touch upon privacy concerns tend to omit considerations of to whom individuals' privacy would be lost, whether they be peers, the state, private companies or hackers. In contrast, discussions of privacy in social media frequently imply that users of, for example, Sesame Credit, run the risk of Ant Financial (and, by extension, Alibaba) accessing more of their personal data than is required for the purpose of credit scoring.

Although most social media references to social credit primarily touch upon questions of how users can raise their scores within commercial products such as Sesame Credit, there is a limited and rich subset of discussions around issues of privacy, personal data protection, and overreach of the system's data gathering. In general, the handful of social media posts addressing privacy concerns in the Social Credit System are more critical of the technology companies providing scores than they are of state-run social credit issuers. At the moment, this may simply reflect that more citizens are familiar with and regularly use the commercial social credit apps than the smaller, local government social credit services. However, this absence of critical comments about government agencies' potential for information abuse may just as well be due to censorship or self-censorship." (Note – or perhaps it's a fear of treading in a sort of no-man's land, with unpredictable – or perhaps even all-too-predictable, risks and consequences!)

"On question-and-answer platforms, online bulletin boards, and web forums, two rare types of netizens are particularly vocal in critiquing the Social Credit System. The first category includes a smattering of individuals who have negative experiences with commercially-provided social credit applications and subsequently feel their privacy has been compromised. The second group comprises self-identified information technology professionals and scholars. They complain about the opacity (opaqueness) of private companies' scoring algorithms, users' inability to access the data companies have stored on them, the absence of repair mechanisms, and a lack of transparency around which third parties can access individuals' personal data and for which purposes.

A few social media users have pointed to the fact that laws addressing some of the problems they have identified do exist, such as protections against credit rating organizations sharing personal data with a third party without first obtaining the data subject's consent. However, they also note that these laws are hardly enforced. Users within both groups have repeated the recommendation that only 'large, trustworthy, law-abiding organizations' should be entrusted with handling personal data. This opinion lends support to the government line that when it comes to massive personal data collection, the state is more likely to protect the public good than private companies are.

In conclusion, the way in which official media talk about the Social Credit System speaks to the fact that the Chinese government is determined to establish this system and views it as essential both for a functioning trust-based economy and to solve a variety of social ills. At the same time, the discussion in both official and social media suggests that the translation of the vision into practice is in flux, and that the Chinese government still has a number of issues to resolve. The question therefore is not if the system will take root, but what it will look like when it fully arrives. The implementation process from 2014 to 2017 provides vital clues to what the system will look like in practice.

D) The State Of Implementation:
Creating A Framework, Experimenting With Pilots

The Social Credit System is a massive and complex project that will require many different government agencies to coordinate their work practices with one another. At the national level, the government has issued plans for division of labor until 2020 covering 12 main areas subdivided into 84 sub-areas of responsibility, all of which are major policy projects requiring a high degree of synchronization. (Citing: NDRC and PBOC 'Division of Tasks for the Social Credit System Construction Plan' (2014-2020) December 16, 2014 – www.ndrc.gov.cn)

The current implementation process can roughly be divided into two tracks: one, creating an overall nationwide framework for assessing both financial credit and moral integrity (new laws and regulations, institutionalizing basic structures for cooperation, setting common standards), and two, experimenting with provincial, sectoral and commercial pilots.

1) The central government's focus:
facilitating cooperation and enforcing blacklists

Currently implementation at the national level centers on ensuring cooperation between different government bureaucracies as well as publicly sanctioning individuals and companies that have been blacklisted for failing to comply with relevant laws and court orders.

Focus 1: Getting different actors to share their data

A large number of bureaucracies are involved in setting up the Social Credit System on the government side. The key to making the Social Credit System work is ensuring proper flow and accessibility of information. One of the greatest roadblocks is getting these different actors to work together to make sure that an individual or entity who has defaulted (or stood out positively) in one area will also be punished (or rewarded) in others. A study on the development of the Social Credit System conducted by Qianhai Credit and the Liaowang Institute (a think tank under the Xinhua news agency) has noted that reduplication of efforts is inevitable, and might impede the progress of the system's establishment if government and private organizations fail to adequately consult with one another and share data. To address this lack of coordination, several mechanisms are currently being put into place.

First, in 2007, the Chinese government set up the Interministerial Conference on Social Credit System Construction as a coordinating body. Headed by the NDRC and the PBOC, it now consists of 46 party and government organs, including players such as the Ministry of Finance and the State Administration for Industry and Commerce on the one hand, and the Ministry of Public Safety and the Central Propaganda Department on the other.

In addition, the Chinese government is currently introducing the Unified Social Credit Number System as a basic prerequisite for different ministries to be able to exchange information with one another. In the past, different bureaucracies used different numbers schemes to identify legal entities. These are now gradually being replaced by a unified 18-digit number to identify natural and legal persons across different bureaucracies and to store all social credit related information on them under a unified number. This step will lay the groundwork for social credit ratings to double as a form of identity, following citizens and companies through multiple aspects of their daily lives as well as across different cities and provinces.

Finally, the actual number of actors involved in establishing the Social Credit System is larger than just the members of the of the Interministerial Conference, as it includes all ministries to some extent, all local governments, industry associations, and commercial players. Therefore, to solve the problem of cooperation, different government and non-government actors have also been signing joint memorandum and memoranda of cooperation focused on how to report data and which punishments to mete out for (social) credit offenders.

Focus 2: Punishment for credit offenders and awards for high scorers

While the Social Credit System is still under construction, blacklists of non-compliant individuals and legal entities (and 'red lists' for outstanding companies and individuals) form the core of the current stage of implementation. The main focus is on punishing offenders on the blacklists, though some measures for rewarding those on red lists have also been passed.

At present, individuals are primarily blacklisted for resisting court orders while companies are blacklisted for breaking existing laws and regulations in a number of areas. The number of offenses resulting in individuals being blacklisted and punished is constantly expanding as ministries and departments come up with additional sectoral regulations for rewards and punishments.

By design of the system, sanctions for loss of creditworthiness have a serious impact on the subject's ability to lead a normal life or pursue their business. For instance, legal representatives of companies that have been blacklisted are no longer allowed to hold a leading position in another company for a number of years or to send their children to private schools.

In addition to the punishments, blacklisting also has reputational cost, as Chinese government agencies are already making these lists publicly available through their databases as well as through major news websites. Naming and shaming through the wide publication of the names, photos, state ID numbers, and in some cases even home addresses of blacklisted persons, is an integral part of this system.

The government has set up two central platforms to make information widely available to the public through a centralized system and to allow queries on blacklisted legal and natural persons. The first is Credit China, a website offering information on the Social Credit System and queries for information on blacklisted persons. The second is the National Enterprise Credit Information Publicity System, which is specifically for companies and allows users to look up information on the company's license, where it is registered, and if it has been blacklisted or listed for irregularities. Naming and shaming is not only seen as unproblematic by Chinese government authorities, but is actually celebrated. For example, several cartoons published on the central government's Credit China platform explain that having one's face and ID number revealed will create social pressure and shame both individuals and companies into adopting more compliant behavior.

In conclusion, while the measures implemented nationwide are still relatively basic, they lay down the groundwork for information gathering and sharing that could later be used to centrally store all kinds of data, including on a person's social network, online behavior and other data points currently only used in pilots. In addition, different government agencies are coordinating to come up with ways to punish social credit offenders. While currently these are only applied to companies breaking certain laws and people defying court orders, the circle of those affected by these punishments may expand in the future.

No uniform standards for credit repair

Mechanisms of credit repair – the appeals process for disputing negative rating data and restoring one's score to good standing – and opportunities for forgiveness of previous infractions, differ by province and sector. Lian Weiliang, a Deputy Director of the National Development and Reform Commission (NDRC) has listed the lack of measures for credit repair as one of four points for improvement in the Social Credit System, signaling regulators' awareness that the system must leave open avenues of redemption. At present, however, there are no uniform standards on credit repair for low social credit scores. Some province-level policies have suggested that volunteer work and donations to charity may serve as legitimate forms of reviving poor social credit ratings. However, policy documents have not yet addressed the problem of long-term reputational damage that comes along with being publicly shamed for what may be relatively minor infractions.

2) Pilot programs: ambitious beta-testing of the system

In addition to measures put in place on a nationwide basis, the Chinese government is actively promoting pilot programs to test out new measures that, if successful, can then be implemented more widely. These pilots can be divided into two types: first, there are government-run local and sectoral pilots, i.e., experiments conducted in individual provinces, cities, or limited to certain policy areas or industries. Second, there are commercial pilots, which allow private companies to test non-mandatory credit scoring schemes. These pilots are the proving grounds for the Social Credit System, as they provide a bellwether for how the system may or may not progress.

Local and sectoral pilots: prototypes of nationwide measures

The majority of provinces have been forging ahead with credit information systems since 2015, and the policies they experiment with are expected to serve as potential prototypes of nationwide measures. Each province has set up leading small groups or interministerial conference systems mirroring the central government to coordinate policy making at the provincial level. Three provinces (Shaanxi, Hubei and Hebei) as well as the provincial-level city of Shanghai have passed regulations for how to handle social credit information. While national legislation is still under way, the NDRC announced in June 2017 that it has fast-tracked research into a legal framework and credit standards, which can then use the provincial regulations for reference.

As is the case with other Chinese policymaking procedures, social credit policy plans have also identified priority areas where the system is to be established and tried out first, with the aim of transferring experience gained when scaling the system up for implementation in other parts of the country. Priority areas are the sectors the Chinese government considers most pressing and where it sees the most urgent need to establish measures to assess market participants' trustworthiness and punish infractions. These include fields such as production, taxes, pricing, healthcare, e-commerce, education and IPR (Intellectual Property Rights).

The State Council has designated a total of 43 municipalities and districts to experiment with new ways to assess credibility and to punish behavior considered illegal or immoral. As provincial plans have progressed, locales have started experimenting with new ways to assess (social) credit and mete out punishments as well. These pilots are where more innovative and advanced developments are taking place, including those that have the greatest potential to violate the privacy or reputational rights of individuals.

For example, since November 2016, the Shanghai Municipal Government has been experimenting with a mobile phone application called Honest Shanghai. Users can input their state ID number and within 24 hours they will receive one of three ratings ('very good,' 'good,' or 'bad') based on government data collected on them. As participation is not mandatory, there are only rewards for individuals with good scores and no punishments for those with bad scores. However, this could change in the future if the scheme becomes mandatory.

Other local pilots, such as Rongcheng in Shandong, have gone further in assigning their residents a score of up to 1000 points, with deductions for infractions such as running a traffic light, and then assigning the person a grade from AAA to D. Depending on the grade, people receive preferential treatment or are burdened with additional requirements when interacting with government bureaucracies.

Some of the pilots test ways to punish people put on blacklists and socially shame them in ways that substantially affect their social and professional lives. For instance, Sanmen County in Zhejiang and Dengfeng County in Henan are testing a measure in which local courts cooperate with telecommunications companies to change the dial tones of individuals refusing to comply with a court order. In this pilot, the court provides telecommunications companies with lists of individuals who have refused to comply with court orders to repay money (including relatively small sums of a few thousand Chinese Yuan). If anybody tries to call them, they will receive a message informing them the person they are trying to reach has been blacklisted and urging the caller to persuade them to honor the court order. The first cases of such ringtones were tested in June of 2017.

Commercial pilots: advanced, but regulatory status remains unclear

Non-mandatory commercial pilots of credit rating schemes are where both the most innovative and most controversial measures are being tested. In order to attract more people, companies such as Ant Financial Services' Sesame Credit offers rewards to users choosing to participate in their credit pilots, such as deposit-free rentals of umbrellas, e-bikes, and even cars. Roughly modeled after FICO scores in the United States or Schufa scores in Germany, Sesame Credit gives users a credit score between 350 and 950, based on a number of criteria including online purchases, demographic details, timely bill payment, and social connections, even though their exact methods of calculating scores remain opaque.

The use of data about users' online behavior, including their social networks, to generate scores to rate their creditworthiness has rightly been identified as having the potential to become a tool for totalitarian surveillance.

However, authorities have sent ambiguous signals about the future of these pilots. The People's Bank of China decided not to grant official licenses to the eight private companies it originally gave permission to conduct social credit pilot testing in 2015, echoing the line of argumentation often found in news and social media that commercial players cannot be trusted. The three reasons the regulator provided for withholding licenses included all eight companies' failure to adequately protect user privacy, over-collection of data deemed irrelevant to credit scoring, and 'conflicts of interest' given that the companies provide e-commerce, fintech, and other services in competition with one another; a potential impediment to the centralized vision of social credit that would require these firms to share their proprietary data with one another. Thus, these pilots' current status as well as their future fate remains unclear: Whether these private platforms will become integrated with the government-run side of the Social Credit System, allowed to continue operating independently or eventually be completely sidelined, is an important open question regarding the future relations of state and private commercial actors in China.

E) The Social Credit System Will Fundamentally Reshape China

The Social Credit System is a policy initiative that addresses several legitimate concerns about the current lack of unified standards and credit rating mechanisms in China, but it also has the potential to go far beyond what we see in other countries in terms of technology-backed societal control. China still struggles with many challenges regarding the standardization and deployment of credit rating mechanisms. But even though many of the current policy measures and mechanisms established on a national level (such as the Unified Social Credit Numbers) are still very basic, they lay the groundwork for a system that can effectively steer the behavior of companies and individuals by making sure that defaulting in one area will be punished across as many other meaningful areas as possible.

Moreover, local, sectoral and commercials pilots experiment with ways to implement the technologically-driven vision for creating a system that combines economic and non-economic factors. Even if only some of the mechanisms currently tested in pilots are adopted nationwide with a functional infrastructure to share data between different ministries and local governments, this would result in a system that would grant the Chinese government massive powers over all natural and legal persons by ensuring that the costs of non-compliance with whatever policy it wishes to enforce are too high to bear.

As the system is taking shape, additional new regulations will be passed, reshaping the business environment of China. This will happen both on the national and provincial levels. Conditions and standards will likely vary across provinces for several years to come, requiring companies operating on the Chinese market to adjust to conditions in the specific jurisdictions where they operate.

Foreign stakeholders should familiarize themselves with the plans published by the Chinese government, keep track of new sectoral and provincial policy developments, and seek clarification from government organs about unclear regulations. While the system is still being set up, there may even be potential for foreign stakeholders to advise the Chinese government on 'best practices' in areas including credit repair and data protection, and have an impact on implementation.

At present, the Chinese government has shown little interest in exporting its Social Credit System to other countries. This is despite the fact that privately owned Chinese mobile payment companies are extending their services outside of the country, providing the data-gathering foundations for spreading their scoring services abroad as well. Although the Chinese government may wish to promote social credit overseas in the future, for the next few years the focus will be on trying to create a functional system domestically.

A new industry may emerge around raising credit ratings as well as (possibly) managing social credit scores. Indeed, by making low scorers' names public through blacklists, the system enables firms and other actors to easily identify and target precisely those individuals and companies seeking a quick boost to their score, through legal and illegal means. However, authorities may come to see commercial rating services and their potential advisory services as competitors, given the troves of personal of person data the former continuously gather from their user bases. Tensions between commercial social credit issuers and their state counterparts, along with regulators who may seek to uphold the latter while supporting the market for the former, will further complicate organic developments of the Social Credit System.

Even though protection of both individuals' privacy and firms' trade secrets are often juxtaposed in official media discussions, it seems unlikely that enforcement of data protection provisions will be up to EU standards in practice or that the business interests of foreign companies will play a major role in setting standards. The challenges of implementing better cybersecurity and data-sharing practices will grow in tandem with the interconnection of the disparate companies, government bureaus, and third-party services that will comprise the social credit system.

At present, bottom-up resistance to the policy initiative seems unlikely, in part because many people seem to agree that there needs to be greater accountability and trust in Chinese society. As more and more individuals' and companies' ratings take on meaningful consequences in everyday life and business affairs, however, citizens and companies are likely to make more vocal demands for clarification of the standards and criteria used to calculate credit scores.

It is more likely that the rivalry between government agencies and large commercial players, which is also reflected in the distrust displayed towards commercial players in official media, may ultimately rein in the unchecked developments of commercial social credit pilots. Private social credit issuers, and China's tech giants in particular, are at an advantage in gathering massive amounts of granular data about citizens and in giving teeth to the blacklisting system by punishing users with low scores. Both of these features make these companies extremely valuable to the state. Yet these providers also rely on regulators leaving them the room to experiment, creating a symbiosis in state-firm relations that could be upset if policymakers clamp down on the pilot tests. As development of the Social Credit System unfolds, this will be the most important relationship to follow."

Note: to a great degree, that the "evolution" of this kind of rivalry between government agencies and large commercial players will be a very significant relationship to follow, is undoubtedly true; but other relationships will also matter a great deal: especially how the relationship between the mass of people and companies and businesses evolves! It is the apparent widespread lack of faith and "trust" in businesses and companies to act "fairly" – to demonstrate goodwill towards the people, and have the basic best interests of the consumers, the mass of people, held high in mind; that stands to a large degree behind this effort to develop a social credit system! And it is the apparent widespread lack of faith and "trust" in people to act honestly, to deal civilly with one another, which is also to a large degree a strong consideration for this effort.

And, though this isn't discussed much, how people are relating to, are viewing their relationship with government – local and central, has to be an underlying concern as well. China, and the Chinese-psyche; its central and more-local governments; how the people relate and deal with so much that is rapidly evolving so quickly; all these have great ramifications socially, politically, and economically; and have to be of great concern to the leaders of China, as well as its people!

Part Five:
A Closer Examination Of Potential Implications

Moving on from a highly detailed examination of the structure and roll-out of the Chinese Social Credit System, we take a closer look at some of the innovative technology involved and the algorithms being used; where this could be taking us – advocators perceived strengths and critics/opponents perceived weaknesses/flaws/dangers of such a social credit system; the implications of more focused government and public surveillance; and potential political, business, social and cultural ramifications.

We begin with an article written by Dom Galeon, ("Futurism" staff writer), and Brad Bergan, (science writer and editor), dated December 2, 2017, and posted on futurism.com, that is titled, "China's 'Social Credit System' Will Rate How Valuable You Are As A Human."

The article begins:

"A Citizen Score In China

In a contentious world first, China plans to implement a social credit system (officially referred to as a Social Credit Score or SCS) by 2020. The idea first appeared in a document from the State Council of China published in June 2014. It is a technological advancement so shocking to modern-minded paradigms that many can do little but sit back in defeatist chagrin as science fiction shows us its darker side.

The SCS seems relatively simple. Every citizen in China, which now has numbers swelling to well over 1.3 billion, would be given a score that, as a matter of public record, is available for all to see. This citizen score comes from monitoring an individual's social behavior – from their spending habits and how regularly they pay bills, to their social interactions – and it'll become the basis of that person's trustworthiness, which would also be publicly ranked.

This actually sounds worse than an Orwellian nightmare.

A citizen's score affects their eligibility for a number of services, including the kinds of jobs or mortgages they can get, and it also impacts what schools their children quality for. In this respect, the SCS resembles one of the most chilling episodes from "Black Mirror's" third season. Incidentally, the show isn't really known as a 'feel-good' flick. It presents various dystopian views of society, but China's SCS proves reality is darker than fiction.

This 'service' isn't slated to go full-swing until 2020, but China has already started a voluntary implementation of the SCS by partnering with a number of private companies in order to iron out the algorithmic details needed for such a large-scale, data-driven system.

The companies that are working in this respect include China Rapid Finance, which is a partner of social network giant Tencent, and Sesame Credit, a subsidiary of Alibaba affiliate company Ant Financial Services Group (AFSG). Both Rapid Finance and Sesame Credit have access to intimidating quantities of data, the former through its WeChat messaging app (at present with 850 million active users) and the latter through its Alipay payment service.

According to local media (www.sohu.com/a/162878300_114778) Tencent's SCS comes with its QQ chat app, where an individual's score comes in a range of between 300 and 850 and is broken down into five sub-categories: social connections, consumption behavior, security, wealth and compliance.

Positive (and Negative) Reinforcement

Proponents of the SCS see this as an opportunity to improve on some of the state's services. Some argue that this would give Chinese citizens much-needed access to financial services. The government also says that this will 'allow the trustworthy to roam everywhere under heaven while making it hard for the discredited to take a single step,' according to the Wall Street Journal (www.wsj.com/articles/chinas-new-tool-for-social-control-a-credit-rating-for-everything-1480351590).

The utopic (utopian) goal of managing citizen finances via structural checks and balances feels like an elegant solution to assuage public debt, and will certainly encourage all involved to improve their debt activity. But structural management of personal finances on this all-pervasive level crosses several boundaries.

The major issue is this: the SCS goes well beyond just rating one's ability to manage debt; in essence, it puts a number on a citizen rating their worth as a human being – and it forces others to respect that rating.

'China's proposed social score is an absolute reaffirmation of China continuing to push forward to be a complete police state, ' said Anurag Lal, former Director of the U.S. National Broadband Task Force for the FCC under the Obama administration and president and CEO of mobility solutions firm Infinite Convergence, in an e-mail to 'Futurism'. 'They take it a step further by becoming not only an establishment of a totalitarian police state that monitors its people, but one that completely evades (invades) users' privacy. All forms of activity and interactions, online or otherwise, will be rated, available to view and stored as data.'

It seems that the infamous Great Firewall" (of China – per Wikipedia: "the combination of legislative actions and technologies enforced by Chinese authorities to regulate the Internet domestically. Its role in the Internet censorship in China is to block access to selected foreign websites and to slow down cross-border Internet traffic. Besides censorship, the Great Firewall has also influenced the development of China's internal Internet economy by nurturing domestic companies and reducing the effectiveness of products from foreign Internet companies") "is only the most well-known feature of China's worsening socio-political plight.

Big Data for Good Behavior

More than working as a social enabler, such a system could end up becoming highly restrictive. Speaking to 'Wired' (www.wired.co.uk/article/chinese-government-social-credit-score-privacy-invasion), Sesame Credit's Technology Director, Li Yingyun, admitted as much, saying that under an SCS system, a person could be judged by his purchases. 'Someone who plays video games for ten hours a day, for example, would be considered an idle person,' Li said. 'Someone who frequently buys diapers would be considered as probably a parent, who on balance is more likely to have a sense of responsibility.'

Some see these as positive developments, by virtue of which a person is encouraged to take greater responsibility for their living and spending habits in order to earn a positive citizen score – i.e. become 'trustworthy.' Chinese blogger Rasul Majid told 'Wired' that he actually thinks it's a better way of keeping tabs on how the government monitors his data. If one knows how one is surveilled, one knows when and where to clean up one's act.

Lal, however, disagrees: 'How do you define people's behaviors on a day-to-day basis? People do so many different things for so many different reasons, and if the context is not appreciated it can be misconstrued,' he said. The words ring true. One does not need to think hard to uncover why it may be problematic to say that people who have children are, in essence, people you should trust. What does that mean for the infertile? What does that mean for same-sex couples? What does it mean for people who simply do not wish to have children?

Probably nothing good.

In the end, even a basic SCS system that only rates a few data points could paint a very inaccurate and incomplete picture of a person. 'You may be playing games for 10 hours and if the algorithm says you're idle, it might miss the reason you're playing these games. Maybe you're an engineer and you're beta testing them. But now you're automatically designated as an idle person,' Lal added. 'When in reality, maybe you were just doing your job.'

Ultimately, the problem is that 'socially acceptable behavior' will be defined by the Chinese government, not a democratic process or an objective panel. And punitive measures will certainly be taken when a person breaks this trust.

With the SCS, the Chinese government will actually hit two birds with one stone: they will have a way of promoting and enforcing what they consider to be 'socially acceptable behavior,' and they will have a way of monitoring virtually all aspects of citizens' lives.

Lal doesn't believe this setup could fly long term though. 'In the free world, this will never catch on. If they're naïve enough to roll it out, it will harm China's credibility on a regional and global scale. Tech companies working in China are already frustrated due to the intense restrictions when it comes to tech policies and encryption – this will only add to their frustration.'

This system represents something more insidious than the panopticon (https://plato.stanford.edu/entries/foucault/#4.4) that renowned social theorist Michel Foucault warned us about. So let's hope that Lal is correct."

Notes of interest: Wikipedia describes panopticon as "a type of institutional building (notably a prison), and a system of control designed by philosopher and social theorist Jeremy Bentham in the late 18th century, in which all parts of the interior are" (and all persons in the interior, are presumed to be) "visible from a single point."

Also: per Wikipedia, Michel Foucault (1926-1984) was a "French philosopher, historian of ideas, social theorist and literary critic. Foucault's theories primarily address the relationship between power and knowledge, and how they are used as a form of social control through societal institutions."

The next article to be reviewed was written by Lund University, Sweden, academicians Stefan Brehm and Nicholas Loubere, dated January 15, 2018, posted on https://phys.org (a science, research and technology news aggregator); and is titled, "China's Dystopian Social Credit System Is A Harbinger Of the Global Age Of The Algorithm."

The article begins:

"The Chinese government's ongoing attempts to create a social credit system aimed at rating the trustworthiness of people and companies have generated equal measures of fascination and anxiety around the world. Social credit is depicted as something uniquely Chinese – a nefarious and perverse digital innovation that could only be conceived of and carried out by a regime like the Chinese Communist party.

The proposed system will draw on data gathered from individuals and businesses to provide social credit scores based on both economic and social behaviour. While government proposals provide little detail about how scores will be calculated, current pilots use both online consumer behaviour and the scores of others in a person's network.

The stated aim is to 'provide the trustworthy with benefits and discipline the untrustworthy ... (so that) integrity becomes a widespread social value'. The official documents are light on detail, but have suggested various ways to punish untrustworthy members of society with low scores, such as through restrictions on employment, consumption, travel, and access to credit.

It is seen as a signal of a dystopian future, but one that could only exist in China's authoritarian context." (Note: but with the spread of authoritarian leaders and governments throughout the world in the latter part of the second decade of the 21st century, is China's more authoritarian system of government becoming more the norm than the exception?) "But China's plans to 'build an environment of trust' – as the Chinese government's State Council puts it – using the data generated from digital activity, is not (need not only be) uniquely Chinese... the country's experiments are a natural extension of a global trend where data is being used to control society.

Pilots underway

The impetus to create a social credit system in China came largely from the country's dearth of a credit rating infrastructure; most people have no credit score. In 2014 the government outlined plans to create a nationwide social credit system by 2020.

Today, the Chinese social credit system is far from unified or centralised. Like most new policies in China, it is being subjected to China's distinctive policy modeling processes. Local governments produce their own interpretations of policies, which then vie to become national models. Currently, over 30 local governments have been piloting social credit systems, using different approaches to arrive at their social credit scores.

In contrast to other policies, however, until recently social credit was also being piloted by eight large Chinese Internet companies. The most well known of these is Alibaba's Sesame Credit, which uses opaque algorithms to arrive at social credit scores for their customers drawn from data provided by an affiliate company called Ant Financial. Those with high scores – the top score is 950 – have been able to access a range of benefits from other Alibaba business and their partners. In mid-2017 the government declined to renew the licenses for the private pilots over conflict of interest concerns. However, the door has been left open for these pilots to be merged into the ongoing attempts to construct a nationwide government-run system.

The expansion of these social credit systems fits neatly into moral and economic narratives that are now prominent in China. These are linked to a perceived 'trust deficit' in the country. High profile cases of economic and social fraud regularly go viral on Chinese social media. This has resulted in a popular discourse of the decline of morality and the inability to trust other people or companies.

Social credit is also presented as a way to improve financial inclusion. Supporters argue that expanding financial services and credit to previously excluded groups is good for socioeconomic development. They believe intrusive methods of assessing creditworthiness are justified in order to reduce the risk to lenders. In this way, Chinese social credit reform mirrors financial inclusion initiatives elsewhere, such as the use of psychometrics (per Wikipedia: "the field in psychology and education that is devoted to testing, measurement, assessment and related activities") and other personal digital data to determine whether someone is eligible for a loan.

Social credit beyond China

Socio-economic credit systems are not confined to China. Most industrialized nations have relied on credit ratings for decades to quantify the financial risks associated with countries, firms and individuals. But social factors are increasingly being included to make more accurate predictions.

In China, Alibaba's Sesame Credit factors in credit scores of a debtor's social network. This means that those with low-score contacts will see a negative impact on their own scores. In the U.S., Affirm, a San Francisco-based lender headed by PayPal co-founder Max Levchin, combs through a wide range of sources, such as social networks, to evaluate the default risk of a creditor. And Lenddo, a Hong Kong-based company, took an even bolder approach and informed debtors' friends on Facebook when they didn't pay installments in time.

So, credit scores based on social action aren't just unique to China and authoritarian regimes. However, this doesn't make them less concerning.

The primary downside of public rating systems like social credit is the far-reaching consequences of low ratings. In China, a recent administrative regulation dictates that defaulting debtors will be listed and shamed on online platforms. Similar measures have taken place in the U.S. The New York Post, for instance, filed a Freedom of Information request and published the performance ratings and names of teachers evaluated by a 'secret algorithm' in an attempt to shame those deemed not to be performing as well.

Rule by algorithms

Experiments repeatedly confirm that data and algorithms are as biased as society is, and reproduce real life segmentation and inequality. In her book the 'Weapons of Math Destruction', American mathematician Cathy O'Neil warned that we need algorithmic audits.

Algorithms that measure social credit and trustworthiness could theoretically be fair – but those in positions of power may well find a way to circumnavigate them. And even though social credit schemes are supposed to extend access to financial resources to previously excluded populations, it's likely that credit solutions driven by big data will exacerbate existing social divides. In the U.S., for example, 45 million Americans do not have a credit score because they lack a credit history, and minority groups and low-income neighbourhoods have a disproportionately high rate of credit invisibility. For China, it's likely something similar could emerge.

Social credit has the potential to cement and exacerbate existent power imbalances in societies, while simultaneously closing down spaces of resistance. The social credit system in development in China is a phenomenon that belongs to a global trend with a transformative potential that is just as threatening in Western democracies. It is but one harbinger of a likely common digital future marked by a shift away from the rule of law and towards rule by algorithms.

Another important article, featuring an interview with the well-known author, Rachel Botsman, is Public Radio International's "What's Your Citizen 'Trust Score'? China Moves To Rate Its 1.3 Billion Citizens." The article was written by Amulya Shankar, dated November 9, 2017 and posted on www. pri.org/stories/

The article begins:

"Take George Orwell's '1984.' Now sprinkle in that episode of 'Black Mirror' where characters live in a world in which every aspect of their lives is dominated by ratings. Chinese officials say it" – the new Social Credit System, with its credit ratings and scoring – "is a way to influence their citizens' behavior to benefit society and move their country forward, but others think it's just the latest step in the country's long history of state surveillance.

Rachel Botsman has written about China's Social Credit System in her book, 'Who Can You Trust? How Technology Brought Us Together and Why It Might Drive Us Apart.' PRI's 'The World' spoke to her about what the plan could look like in 2020.

How a person's rating could be calculated:

Ms. Botsman: 'The Social Credit System – I guess we would probably call it, like, a 'National Trust Score' – will look at different dimensions of a person's life. So things that you might expect, like whether you pay your bills on time or your mortgage. But also your purchasing patterns, things that you say on social media and whether those things conform with the government. Where it gets, I think, very 1984, is it will look at the patterns and the behavior of your friends and your social connections as well.'

The kind of behavior that could bring a person's score down:

Ms. Botsman: 'Well I think there's behavior that you'd expect – if you make a fraudulent payment or something like that – but then there are things that are more subtle. For example, if you buy work shoes or diapers, you could be seen as a responsible citizen and your score might go up. But if you're buying lots of video games your score will maybe go down, because people would think that you're lazy. If you happen to post something on Tiananmen Square, that is likely to negatively impact your score. This goes beyond the way we think about traditional credit scores, and really gets into your character in a way that is quite frightening.'

The potential perks of having a high 'trust score', and the consequences of a low 'trust score':

Ms. Botsman: 'The benefits are really interesting, everything from being fast-tracked to visas, to getting discounts on hotels, or car rental, or insurance policies. The part that worries me is in fact the penalties, because if your trust score goes below a certain level, it could impact everything from where your children go to school, to what jobs you can apply for, and the type of mortgage that you can get. Your transgressions, they will follow you forever – it is really a permanent record of your so-called trustworthiness. So your behavior could impact your children or your grandchildren for decades to come. There seems to be no limits, there seems to be no boundaries, as to how far this can go.'

The Chinese government's reasons for (fully) implementing the Social Credit Score in 2020:

Ms. Botsman: 'The government's justification is both economic and social. So the reason why they're saying they need this is because just doing business in China can be hard. You know, when I interviewed people from China on this, they don't necessarily see this as a bad thing, because many people in China do not have traditional credit scores, those sort of traditional gold standards of trust. And it's also so culturally embedded in the way they live. So they'll say in their grandparents' generation (people) knew that the Communist Party had a file on them, but they had no idea what was in that file. This is actually the same system. Digitized, but it's more transparent.'

The big picture:

Ms. Botsman: 'This particular chapter, it was one of the hardest pieces of the book to get right, because it's really easy to take a Western lens. It's really easy to point our finger at China without stopping and actually saying, 'well how far is this culture of surveillance from the West?' It sounds like completely nightmarish territory that the West would never descend into, in terms of using these trust algorithms that are fairly reductive about people.

But then when you really look into the amount of data that companies are collecting, and how they're using that data to get a complete picture of how we behave, where we are at any given time, what our political views are – we're not that far off. It's just that the government doesn't own that data. And this is another point you hear from the Chinese people – that it isn't so far off in the West, it's just that you have no control, because it's a black box system!

There's a part of me that accepts that this notion of privacy is dead. And this idea that we're in control of the data that we post online and where it goes – I just think that's an ignorant position to take."

Another article that covers some now familiar ground, but adds some new dimensions as well, is John Harris' article written for The Guardian (www.theguardian.com), dated March 5, 2018, and is titled "The Tyranny Of Algorithms Is Part Of Our Lives: Soon They Could Rate Everything We Do" and is subtitled "Credit scores already control our finances. With personal data being increasingly trawled, our politics and our friendships will be next."

The article begins:

"For the past couple of years a big story about the future of China has been the focus of both fascination and horror. It is all about what the authorities in Beijing call 'social credit', and the kind of surveillance that is now within governments' grasp. The official rhetoric is poetic. According to the documents, what is being developed will 'allow the trustworthy to roam everywhere under heaven while making it hard for the discredited to take a single step'.

As China moves into the newly solidified President Xi Jinping era, the basic plan is intended to be in place by 2020. Some of it will apply to businesses and officials, so as to address corruption and tackle such high-profile issues as poor food hygiene. But other elements will be focused on ordinary individuals, so that transgressions such as dodging transport fares and not caring sufficiently for your parents will mean penalties, while living the life of a good citizen will bring benefits and opportunities.

Online behaviour will inevitably be a big part of what is monitored, and algorithms will be key to everything, though there remains doubts about whether something so ambitious will ever come to full fruition. One of the schemes basic aims is to use a vast amount of data to create individual ratings, which will decide people's access – or lack of it – to everything from travel to jobs.

The Chinese notion of credit – or xinyong – has a cultural meaning that relates to moral ideas of honesty and trust. There are up to 30 local social credit pilots run by local authorities, in huge cities such as Shanghai and Hangzhou and much smaller towns. Meanwhile, eight ostensibly private companies have been trialing a different set of rating systems, which seem to chime with the government's controlling objectives.

The most high-profile system is Sesame Credit – created by Ant Financial, an offshoot of the Chinese online retail giant Alibaba. Superficially, it reflects the western definition of credit, and looks like a version of the credit scores used all over the world, invented to belatedly allow Chinese consumers the pleasures of buying things on tick, and manage the transition to an economy in which huge numbers of people pay via smartphones. But its reach runs wider.

Using a secret algorithm, Sesame Credit constantly scores people from 350 to 950, and its ratings are based on factors including considerations of 'interpersonal relationships' and consumer habits. Bluntly put, being friends with low-rated people is bad news. Buying video games, for example, gets you marked down. Participation is voluntary but easily secured, thanks to an array of enticements. High scores unlock privileges such as being able to rent a car without deposit, and fast-tracked European visa applications. There are also romantic benefits: the online dating service Baihe gives people with good scores prominence on its platforms.

Exactly how all this will relate to the version of social credit eventually implemented is unclear: licences that might have enabled the systems to be rolled out further ran out last year. There again, Ant Financial has stated that it wants to 'help build a social integrity system' – and the existing public and private pilots have a similar sense of social control, and look set to feed the same social divisions. If you are mouldering away (slipping/dropping) towards the bottom of the hierarchies, life will clearly be unpleasant. But if you manage to be a high-flyer, the pleasures of fast-tracking and open doors will be all yours, though even the most fleeting human interaction will give off the crackle of status anxiety.

It would be easy to assume none of this could happen here in the west. But the 21st century is not going to work like that. These days credit reports and scores – put together by agencies whose reach into our lives is mind-boggling – are used to judge job applications, thereby threatening to lock people into financial problems. And in the midst of the great deluge of personal data that comes from our online lives, there is every sign of these methods being massively extended.

Three years ago Facebook patented a system of credit rating that would consider the financial histories of people's friends. Opaque innovations known as e-scores are used by increasing numbers of companies to target their marketing, while such outfits as the already infamous Cambridge Analytica trawl people's online activities so as to precisely target political messaging. The tyranny of algorithms is now an inbuilt part of our lives.

These systems are sprawling, often randomly connected, and often beyond logic. But viewed from another angle, they are also the potential constituent parts of comprehensive social credit systems, awaiting the moment at which they will be glued together. That point may yet come, thanks to the ever-expanding reach of the internet. If our phones and debit cards already leave a huge trail of data, the so-called internet-of-things is now increasing our informational footprint at speed.

In the short term, the biggest consequences will arrive in the field of insurance, where the collective pooling of risk is set to be supplanted by models that focus tightly on individuals. Thanks to connected devices, insurers could soon know how much television you watch, whether you always obey traffic signals, and how well your household plumbing works. Already, car insurance schemes offer lower premiums if people install tracking devices that monitor their driving habits; and health insurance companies such as the British firm Vitality offer deals based on access to data from fitness trackers. In the near future, as with Sesame Credit, people will presumably sign up for surveillance-based insurance in their droves because of such simple incentives, and those squeamish about privacy may simply have to pay more. Many people, of course, will simply be deemed impossible to protect.

Personal data and its endless uses form one of the most fundamental issues of our time, which boils down to the relationship between the individual and power, whether exercised by government or private organisations. It speaks volumes that in Whitehall responsibility for such things falls uncertainly between the culture secretary, Matt Hancock, whose 'digital' brief includes what the official blurb limply calls 'telecommunications and online', the Treasury, and an under-secretary of state in the business department, Andrew Griffiths, whose portfolio takes in 'consumers'.

That is absurd, and it may yet play its part in our rapid passage into a future that could materialise in both east and west, in which we do what we're told, avoid the company of undesirables – and endlessly panic about how the algorithms will rate us tomorrow."

This Examination Of China's Social Credit System Brought To A Close

Clearly there are positives and negatives to the introduction of such a comprehensive social credit system to China and its people; as well as the possibility, even probability, that such a system could be setting a real-world example for the global community. Indeed, a key area of concern focuses on the possibility, perhaps even the probability, of such a system being the basis for authoritarian/totalitarian "Big Brother" surveillance and control taken to a very high level.

But then again, perhaps the perceived need for, and actual implementation of, such a system, can be seen, can be taken, as an early warning sign/signal that we all need to be much more aware of: that as our world has grown smaller in terms of "connectedness", and our population has grown so much larger, people are having a difficult time finding their ways, their places, in this modern world! People are coming into more contact with other people about whom they actually know very little – in many cases, people have left, been uprooted from, their familiar villages, communities, neighborhoods, towns, to go to cities, which are themselves parts of even larger entities; and they do many things over the computer and the Internet, without even direct human contact. In these changing circumstances and new environments, how, where, do people find other people and businesses to place their trust in? As important, how they find ways to avoid those people and businesses who/that are not honest and trustworthy in their dealings with others? These are, these have to be, among people's major concerns in this modern world of ours!

A comprehensive social credit system like China's is one solution; and in fact, perhaps a suitable one for the history and culture of China and its people. And its substantial focus on holding people accountable and responsible for their actions, and giving people the means, even a public forum, to have their voices heard about matters of trustworthiness, fairness, honesty and even justice, in social, business, and even governmental matters, has to be considered a positive development, even if somewhat rough-edged in real-world actualization.

Yes, these are valid concerns about social credit systems, when a person expresses worries about such systems being used to conduct personal vendettas against other people or businesses; when such systems are used for political gain at the expense of others, and/or to gain competitive edges against other businesses.

Yes, these are valid real-world concerns, when we worry about people gaming the systems to improve their scores; and worry about hackers breaking into the connected systems for personal gain or advantage, or to provide advantages for others. And we are rightly concerned, because it's common knowledge that staying ahead technologically, and technically, of those with bad intentions on the Internet or in computer hardware and software systems, is a never-ending battle!

Out of all these concerns, comes some certainty: that for a social credit system to really work there must be an efficient, effective and timely, as well as a fair and trustable, likely-judicial-based, appeals process!

What this all means is that there's a very strong need to respond to, to find a good and effective response to, people finding that the modern world they find themselves in, is lacking in many ways; isn't providing them the things and feelings they believe they want and need! That real-world, to a large extent, what they basically want and need is to be able to find a safe, secure place for themselves and their loved ones in this modern and rapidly changing world of ours! That real-world, something better, more suitable, needs to be offered to so many people who need help finding honesty and trust in their world; who need help feeling that they're part of something bigger – and better, in this world of ours! And that real-world, perhaps a social credit system, whether like China's, or a considerably less invasive one, could be a good, could be a suitable place, to begin making very desirable changes, in moral, personal, and social interactions of all kinds, on all levels; in this modern-day, 21st century world of ours!

Printed in Great Britain
by Amazon